REVELATION:
God's Blueprint for the Future

Robert Wigley

Published by

IN HIS STEPS PUBLISHING
6500 Clito Road
Statesboro, Georgia 30461 (U.S.A.)

ISBN: 1-58535-205-5

Contents

Dedication

I would like to dedicate this book
to my four grandchildren:

Madison McArthur
Marlee McArthur
Nate Williams
Owen Williams

The Ten Virgins

There were ten virgins in their chamber on that day,
As they waited for the groom to take the bride away.
They knew He would come but they knew not when.
His coming was sure and on that they could depend.
Their lamps had been filled and trimmed with care,
But five were foolish for they had no oil to spare.
The other five were wise, they had plenty to spare.
The oil was for their lamps, they could not share.
As they set in their chamber waiting for the groom,
The oil in their lamps would be gone very soon.
When their oil got low the foolish began to fret.
They would have to leave for precious oil to get.
They left the chamber hoping for some oil to find.
Maybe they would see someone who would be kind.
The others stayed in the chamber, they were prepared.
They knew the groom would come and not be deterred.
When the groom came knocking at the door that night,
The wise virgins were ready for they had plenty of light.
The five that were wise were those that were received.
The wise were prepared but the foolish were deceived.
Have you prepared your lamp for the groom's return?
Is your lamp filled with oil which you cannot earn?
The oil that you must have the Lord will provide.
This oil is free for everyone but you must decide.
Come to Christ and He will give you His Precious oil.
Do not be like other souls and for worldly things toil.

Written by John David Harrell
February 6, 2010

Introduction to the Book of Revelation

The book of Revelation is probably the least read and understood section of the Bible. The average Bible reader knows very little of its contents or meaning.

The basic reason for the neglect of this great prophecy is that most people don't have a solid grasp of the Old Testament. There are some 350 references or allusions to the Old Testament in the Book of Revelation.

Many think the book is too hard to understand. The very title contradicts that idea. The Greek word for—*Revelation* is—*apocalypses*, which means—*to unveil or reveal.*

The Lord commanded that the book be read to the churches (Revelation 22:16). This would be a waste of time if it could not be understood.

The book is unique in that it presents Jesus Christ as He is today. Revelation makes it plain that the Lord's side will have ultimate victory. It will help us to understand what is ahead for this confused planet.

It is the only book that tells us what will happen to the devil. His final destination is the lake of fire (Revelation 20:10). No wonder Satan hates this prophecy.

The key verse is Revelation 1:19–*Write the things which thou hast seen, and the things which are, and the things which shall be hereafter.* The things—*which thou hast seen,* is Chapter One. The —*things which are,* refers to Chapters Two and Three, or—*the Church Age.* The things—*which shall be* includes Chapters Four through Twenty-Two. You can easily see that most of the book is prophetic.

The Book of Revelation completes Bible truth. It can be compared to the Book of Genesis. In Genesis, we see Paradise Lost. In Revelation, we see Paradise Regained. We are going to get back all that Adam lost.

Genesis reveals a curse that came because of man's sin (Genesis 3:17, 18). Revelation explains that the curse will be lifted (Revelation 22:3). We see Satan for the first time in Genesis. We see him for the last time in Revelation. A great old preacher once said, "Thank God that the devil is not mentioned in the first two chapters nor the last two chapters of the Bible."

"The Things Which Thou Hast Seen"

Introduction (verses 1-3) – The very first verse identifies John as the human author of this great book. He is also the author of four other new Testament books—the Gospel of John, and I, II, and III John.

A great blessing is promised in the third verse: *"Blessed is he that readeth, and they that hear the words of this prophecy, and keep those things which are written therein: for the time is at hand."* Divine favor is promised to those who read, hear, and keep the things found in this prophecy.

I. A Message From Heaven (verses 4-11)

We are given greetings from the Father, Son, and Holy Spirit (verses 4-5). Some have been puzzled by the reference to the seven Spirits. There are not seven Holy Spirits. This would make nine members of the Godhead. The Holy Spirit has a sevenfold ministry. These seven characteristics are identified in Isaiah 11:2.

John tells us some wonderful things about Jesus in this passage. He is the *"first begotten of the dead"* (verse 5). The Apostle Paul described Him as *"the first fruits of them that slept"* (I Corinthians 15:20). The Bible records the fact that others may have been restored to life, but Jesus is the first to be truly resurrected. All the others eventually returned to the grave. The Lord Jesus boldly declared that He has *"the keys of hell and of death"* (Revelation 1:18).

Another promise that has given hope for the future is verse seven: *"Behold, He cometh with clouds; and every eye shall see Him, and they also which pierced Him."* This verse corresponds to an Old Testament passage in Zechariah 12:10. It refers to his Second Coming in glory. It is not a description of the Rapture. The Jewish people will finally recognize Him

dge Him as their Messiah: "*All Israel shall be*
...s 11:26).

...s is also referred to as the "*Alpha and*
Omega" (verse 8). These were the first and last letters of the
Greek alphabet. They would correspond to our letters A and
Z. A little girl once explained it this way: "*He is the A and Z*
and all the letters in between!"

John did not see himself as some kind of super-saint. He
was our "*brother*" and "*companion in tribulation*" (verse 9).
Jesus said we would all have to deal with tribulation in this
world (John 16:33).

The elderly apostle had been exiled to the lonely island
of Patmos (verse 9). It was a small island in the Aegean Sea.
It was one of the many isolated places to which the Romans
banished their prisoners. It is important to remember that he
was there because he had remained faithful to God's Word.
He received prison, not prosperity.

John was "*in the Spirit on the Lord's day*" (verse 10).
God spoke to him and directed him to send a book to the
seven churches in Asia (verse 11). These seven churches will
receive personal messages in the next two chapters. This area
where the churches were located is modern-day Turkey.

II. A Messenger From Heaven (verses 12-20)

A marvelous description of the glorified Christ is given
in verses 13-16. He is seen, not as a little baby in swaddling
clothes, not a young man in the carpenter's shop, nor even on
a cross. He is clothed with majesty and power. This picture is
far different than the modern conception of Jesus.

John was one of the Lord's *inner circle* during His
earthly ministry. However, when the aged apostle saw Jesus
in His glorified state, he fell at His feet as though he was
dead (verse 17). When we see the Lord in all His glory, we
will realize how unworthy we are. Isaiah had this same reac-
tion. When he saw the Lord high and lifted up, he cried out,

"woe is me" (Isaiah 6:5).

The Lord Jesus reminds us that He has all power and authority: *"I am He that liveth, and was dead; and behold, I am alive forevermore, Amen; and have the keys of hell and of death"* (verse 18). Christianity is the only religion that has a founder who "was dead", but is alive forever. He is the victor over death, a most feared enemy. Since He has the keys to eternity, we can confidently face tomorrow.

We are introduced here to the seven churches which will be representative of the Church Age. We must note that the Church Age begins with Jesus in the midst (verse 13). By the end of this period of time, He will be outside the church and knocking, trying to gain entrance (Revelation 3:20).

Conclusion: This chapter concludes the first part of the outline of the book *"the things which thou hast seen"* (verse 19).

The Roman authorities thought they were getting rid of John by exiling him to a small island. God outsmarted the devil; however, by giving the aged apostle a glorious vision of future events. We can calm our anxious souls by understanding that our God is still in control. God's purposes will never be altered by the devil's trickery.

"Letters to the Seven Churches" – Revelation 2 & 3

Introduction – This is the second division of the book, according to Revelation 1:19. These two chapters define *"the things which are"* or the present church age. The number seven occurs frequently in the book. We will now be introduced to seven churches. We will later see seven seals, seven trumpets, and seven vials of wrath.

There were more than seven churches in John's day, but these churches would be typical of others throughout the centuries. They were located in Asia Minor or present-day Turkey. Islam is the dominant religion in that area of the world today. The Lord usually began by commending the church for its good qualities and then He would explain how they needed to improve. Each letter closes with an encouragement to the *"overcomers."* We must not think the "overcomers" were some kind of super-saints. *"For whatsoever is born of God overcometh the world: and this is the victory that overcometh the world, even our faith. Who is he that overcometh the world, but he that believeth that Jesus is the Son of God?"* (I John 5:4,5).

"Ephesus: Losing Your First Love"

I. The Church at Ephesus (2:1-7)

"Unto the angel of the church" (verse 1). Each letter will be addressed to "the angel of the church." The word for "angel" means "messenger." Some think it refers to the pastor. Ephesus means "desired ones." The story of how this church began can be found in Acts 19.

"Seven stars" and "seven candlesticks" are also mentioned in the first verse. Their identity is revealed in Revelation 1:20. The "seven stars" are the messengers and the "seven candlesticks" are the churches themselves.

A. Commendation

Verse 2 – *"I know thy works…labour."* The Lord knows all about us. This was a working church. We are not saved by works, but to do works. A person who doesn't work may not be saved because *"faith without works is dead"* (James 1:22). If a man says he believes in Jesus and never does anything, he is just kidding himself. The word "believe" comes from an English word "bi-live." What a man believes he lives by, all else is just talk.

"Thy patience." They didn't quit working. "Patience" means "endurance." They would not faint or give up easily. You tell the size of a Christian by what it takes to stop him. A woman had a maid who didn't do anything fast but get tired. We have church folks that get tired too quickly (I Corinthians 15:58).

"Canst not bear…evil." This church hated sin. How we need churches today who hate sin and fight it.

"Church" is the Greek word "ecclesia", which means "called out ones." A true church is in the world but not of the world. The early church practiced discipline, but it is almost unheard of today. Some churches today are so worldly that you have to backslide to be in fellowship.

"Tried them which say...Apostles...found them liars." "Apostle" means "one sent from God." They put professors to the test and if they found them deceivers they refused to let them teach or preach. The Bible says to try the spirits and not be led astray by every false wind of doctrine.

Today many churches will call a pastor if he has a seminary degree even though he doesn't believe in the virgin birth, second coming, etc. Sadly, many church members don't know if their preacher is preaching the gospel or not.

The current church needs to heed this message because there are many false apostles disguised as servants of Christ. We have every right to test men to see if they are sent from God. If not, they should be rejected.

Verse 3. He repeats the mention of patience and faithfulness. This seems to have been a marvelous church, but there is a "nevertheless" in the next verse.

B. Condemnation

Verse 4. *"Thou has left thy first love."* Christ is faithful in pointing out our weaknesses as well as our strengths. There was only one flaw, but it was serious.

They did not love the Lord as they once did. This is a danger for every Christian today. The honeymoon was over. Someone said the honeymoon was the time between "I do" and "you better." Love must either grow or decline. It cannot remain static.

Do you remember when you were first married? This loss of love can happen spiritually. We sing, *"every day with Jesus is sweeter than the day before,"* but most don't mean it.

No matter what you do in church, unless it is motivated by love, it does no good (I Corinthians 13). How many times do we do things because we ought to or somebody has to? The primary requirement for a teacher is not love for boys and girls, but for Jesus Christ. Their devotion had grown cold. The honeymoon was over. If you don't love Jesus more than when you were saved, you are backslidden.

C. Counsel

The Lord gives the remedy for their lack of commitment in verse five. It basically comes down to the "three R's"--remember, repent, and repeat (do the first works). They were urged to return back to their first love.

This church hated the deeds of the Nicolaitans (verse 6). This term will be defined in our study of the church at Pergamos (2:15).

Conclusion: The Lord closes this letter with a warning and an encouragement. If they did not repent, He threatened to *"remove thy candlestick"* (verse 5). This doesn't mean they could lose their salvation. It refers to the church as an assembly. A local church congregation can dwindle away to nothing. God will remove His power and anointing.

The Church at Ephesus did lose its candlestick. The Muslims control that city today. The light of the gospel was taken away. The same thing could happen to our nation.

The overcomers were promised that they could eat of the tree of life (verse 7). Adam was forbidden to eat of this tree (Genesis 3:24). Thus, we learn the grand truth that eating will take place in Heaven (Revelation 22:2).

Ephesus represents all the churches who believe the right things, but have no burning enthusiasm for the work of God. They accepted correct doctrines, but their love had grown stale. Ephesus is known as *"The Backsliding Church."*

"Smyrna - The Persecuted Church"

II. The Church at Smyrna (2:8-11)

Introduction - It is interesting to know that one of the seven churches would be dealing with persecution. This may seem hard for some Americans to understand, but most of the world is suffering religious persecution. I am afraid that our religious freedom will not last much longer The entire world is on a course to meet the Antichrist.

I. The Poor Rich Church (Verse 8).

This is the shortest message of the seven churches. The longest was Thyatira. This is one of only two churches that the Lord did not find fault (the other was Philadelphia). We are not to think that these were perfect churches. The local assemblies of believers will always have faults. Those poor souls who are looking for the "perfect church" are wasting their time.

"Unto the angel of the church in Smyrna" (verse 8). The word "Smyrna" means "myrrh." It was a fragrance used in embalming the dead. Myrrh had to be crushed to give its fragrance. It was one of the gifts of the Wise Men (Matthew 2:11).

The church at Smyrna was being crushed by their enemies. The lost world was trying to crush the Christianity out of them. The devil's crowd is using the same tactic today over much of the globe.

The Lord Jesus assured the suffering saints that He knew how they felt. *"These things saith the first and the last, which was dead, and is alive"* (verse 8). He reminded them of His resurrection power. He tells them that He rose from the dead and they will also. Because He lives, we can face the future with confidence.

II. The Sufferings of the Saints (Verses 9-11)

They were facing tribulation because of their faith in Christ (verse 9). This doesn't sound like the prosperity gospel being preached today in America. *"All that will live godly in Christ Jesus shall suffer persecution"* (II Timothy 3:12). *"The servant is not greater than his Lord. If they have persecuted me, they will also persecute you"* (John 15:20).

There were some in the church who were of the "synagogue of Satan" (verse 9). They claimed to be the people of God, but they were imposters. We would call them hypocrites. Thus, we see that the Church at Smyrna was not perfect.

They were to have *"tribulation ten days"* (verse 10). During the time of Roman persecution there were ten decrees or commands which ordered Christians to be put to death. Millions were tormented and killed because of their allegiance to Christ. In those days it meant something to be a believer.

The Lord commanded His followers to be *"faithful unto death"* (verse 10). They were not just to be faithful until things got better. They were not to be faithful until they got tired or retired, but expired.

Conclusion: The overcomers are promised that they would not experience the *"second death"* (verse 11). The Bible defines two kinds of death--physical and spiritual. Physical death is the separation of the soul from the body (James 2:26). Spiritual death, or the "second death", is the separation of both the soul and body from Almighty God (Revelation 20:14). Those who experience the "second death" will be tormented forever in the lake of fire. It will happen to all whose names are not recorded in the book of life. If you have accepted Christ into your heart and been "born again", you won't have to worry about this.

III. "Pergamos—The Church in a Bad Neighborhood" (Revelation 2:12-17)

Introduction - The devil uses many devices in his never-ending attempt to destroy the Church. He used persecution against the saints at Smyrna. He employs a completely different tactic at Pergamos.

The danger at Pergamos was far more subtle. Compromise with the world was the new strategy used by the evil one.

I. Congratulations (Verses 12-13)

"To the angel of the Church in Pergamos" (verse 12). The word "Pergamos" means "marriage." It is concerned with the marriage of the church and the world. The devil's philosophy seems to be, "If you can't beat them, join them."

A great many churches today are using worldly methods in an attempt to expand their membership. Multitudes have the idea that if something works in the world that it will also work in the church.

This church was located in a bad neighborhood. *"I know thy works and where thou dwellest, even where Satan's seat is"* (verse 13). The Lord says, "I know where you are living." He knows the conditions we face daily. If you are surrounded by heathen folks, don't complain. The Lord may have you there for a reason. The people who live or work around you may not go to church. You might be the only *"Jesus"* they will see.

This world is the devil's neighborhood anyway. He is described as *"the god of this world"* (II Corinthians 4:4). We must live <u>in</u> the world, but not be <u>of</u> the world. The world will pass away, but he that does the will of God will abide forever (I John 2:17).

Antipas was the pastor at Pergamos. He was put to

death because he wouldn't go along with the worldly crowd. God calls him a *"faithful martyr"* (Verse 13). The word "martyr" means "witness." The name "Antipas" means "against all." Most likely, he stood his ground and refused to water-down his beliefs. A true child of God will always be in the minority when it comes to ethical concerns.

The finest compliment for a child of God is to be called "a faithful witness." I long to hear the Master say, *"Well done, thou good and faithful servant"* (Matthew 25:21).

II. Condemnation (Verses 14-15)

The Lord saw two things that disturbed him in this church. First, there were some there that held the doctrine of Balaam. Second, there were those who accepted the doctrine of the Nicolaitines. They both are still around today, but under different names.

To understand the beliefs of Balaam, we must familiarize ourselves with Numbers 22-31. Balaam was a popularity-seeker who encouraged the Israelites to intermarry with the Moabites. This was identical to the church at Pergamos. They held the correct views about the Lord, but they failed to separate themselves from the world. There's an old saying that "if you give the devil an inch, he will take a mile."

The Nicolaitines are mentioned in verse 15. This doctrine comes from the blending of two words. "Nikao" means "to conquer" and "laos" means "the people or laity." We all know what a layman is. The meaning here is that there should be a division in the church—clergy and laity. People even have the idea that the clergy (preacher) should dress differently from ordinary members. You hear people exclaim, "You can't do that, you're a preacher." It takes just as much of the grace of God to save a layman as it does a clergyman.

There are two extremes here that we must watch carefully. The preacher is not just "one of the boys", but neither is he to be set on a pedestal. We are to honor and respect our pastors (I Thessalonians 5:13), but we must realize they are saved by grace just like anyone else.

III. Comfort (Verse 17)

The closing has to do with comfort. Christ promises three things to the overcomer--eat of the hidden manna, receive a white stone, and a new name will be brought to light.

The children of Israel were sustained by manna in their wilderness journey. The manna was a picture of the Lord Jesus, The Bread of Life (John 6:48). If the manna was sufficient, the "hidden manna" will be even better. The "white stone" was a symbol of hospitality and friendship. Friends would break a stone in two and carve their names on each half. They would carry the stone in their pocket to remind them of one another.

There is also a secondary application of the "white stone." It was also used as a token that a person would be found innocent after a trial. Those who are resting in Christ will also be found "not guilty" as they stand before the judgment.

The *"new name"* does not mean that we will get another identity in the next world. It means that we will have a "new name" for God. Now we know Him as Savior. Then, we will know Him as Friend. If you want that "new name", don't look on the internet, just give Him your heart.

Conclusion: The church at Pergamos warns us of the dangers of letting the world into the church. When we do that, it won't take long for the message to become diluted. Stand fast, even if you live in a bad neighborhood.

"Thyatira--The Influence of False Teaching" (Revelation 2:18-29)

Introduction - This was the longest letter of the seven churches. All of the places probably seem the same to us, but Thyatira was a small place. The main importance of the city was because of a plant that grew there. It had a purple root and became the main ingredient of a dye that was well-known back then. Paul's first European convert was a seller of purple from Thyatira (Acts 16:14).

This church may have been on the list in order to encourage those pastors in small places. Nearly 80% of all preachers serve congregations of less than 200 members.

I. Praise (Verses 18-19)

"Unto the angel of the church in Thyatira" (verse 18). "Thyatira" means "continual sacrifice." The name tells us they had a doctrinal problem since Jesus completed the work of salvation on the cross.

The Lord commends the good things they were doing (verse 19). This is a needed example for us. We need to begin by looking for the good in a church or in an individual.

II. Problem (Verses 20-23)

The church at Thyatira had a woman who was teaching false doctrine. The Lord identifies her as *"Jezebel"* (verse 20). She considered herself as a "prophetess" and had accumulated a large number of followers. Her supporters were probably young converts with little discernment.

Most likely "Jezebel" was not her real name. She had a similar personality to the Jezebel of the Old Testament. The original Jezebel was very strong-willed and even intimidated the prophets of God, including Elijah (I Kings 19).

Someone in the church was teaching in error. It happened to be a woman. It could just as easily have been a man. The problem was that the church didn't want to deal with it. They were afraid to rock the boat.

The same thing happens so often today. Someone is teaching false doctrine, but the pastor and deacons try to sweep the problem under the rug. They are afraid it will split the church if they try to deal with it. Church discipline is just about obsolete these days. This is why the church's testimony is minimal.

Please note that none of the letter was addressed to Jezebel personally. It was addressed to the church. God rebuked the church for tolerating evil within their fellowship.

Many preachers avoid this passage for fear that it would appear to be someone in their church. A Bible scholar once wrote an article about this text in a church magazine. He received several letters from people who felt they had been personally attacked.

III. Promises (Verses 24-29)

The Lord encourages the true believers to *"hold fast"* (verse 25). The overcomers are promised authority over the nations (verses 26 and 27). This refers to influence in the coming millennial kingdom which will be ruled with *"a rod of iron."* Overcomers are also promised *"the morning star"* (verse 28). The "morning star" is another name for Jesus (Revelation 22:16).

Conclusion: There are a couple of practical lessons in this scripture. First, major church conflicts can originate in small places. Second, smooth-talking people can be leading folks astray. If a person can't back up their message from the Bible, they should be rejected. God's Word is the final authority.

"Sardis - The Dead Church" (Revelation 3:1-6)

Introduction - A dead church does a great deal of harm to the cause of Christ. It seems to be a contradiction in terms because one primary characteristic of a born-again Christian is life (John 10:10).

This is the worst thing that could happen to our local assemblies--to be pronounced dead by the Divine Coroner.

I. Deception (Verse 1)

"Unto the angel of the church in Sardis" (verse 1). "Sardis" means "a remnant" or "those who come out." It is obvious that the church had an acceptable name.

This was all on the surface, however. The Lord explained *"that thou hast a name that thou livest and art dead."* This is the briefest congratulation of any of the seven churches.

Why does a church die? There are no doubt many reasons. They include:

(1) The church remembers where it has been rather than where it's going. Their favorite words include the statement, "it used to be". It's good to learn from the past, but we don't need to live there.

(2) The church cares more for tradition than for evangelism. We must never change our message, but we may have to change methods. Most church folks' favorite phrase is "we've never done it that way before."

If we forget the "great commission" (Matthew 28:19,20), we have no reason to exist. The primary focus of the Lord Jesus was "to seek and to save that which was lost" (Luke 19:10).

(3) The church is dead or dying when it has no concern for the youth and children. They represent what the church will be after we are gone. I have spoken in lots of churches where there are no young people. It will cost something to

have a youth ministry, but it will cost much more if we don't.

The church at Sardis was dead, but didn't know it. They were still going through religious rituals, but with no results for eternity.

II. Advice (Verses 2 and 3)

Our God is in the resurrection business. He delights to bring life where there was death. He tells them to *"be watchful"* (verse 2). The Greek here means to "chase sleep." They needed to "wake-up." This sounds like good advice for the contemporary church.

They were advised to *"strengthen the things which remain"* (verse 2). God is saying, "save the remains." What our churches need is to "save what is left" by repenting and having an old-fashioned revival. If this doesn't happen, we may as well bury the remains.

Jesus will come *"as a thief"* to those not watching for Him (verse 3). One of the best ways to revive a dead church is to get them to be looking for the Lord to come. It will also help free us from the burdens of this old world.

III. Remnant (Verse 4)

A "dead church" label doesn't mean that 100% of the fellowship is lifeless. There were a few in Sardis that were living holy lives (verse 4). I have met some fine people in "dead churches." Many of them are hoping that the church will experience a spiritual renewal and get back on track.

IV. Security (Verse 5)

The Lord promises the overcomers that *"I will not blot out his name out of the book of life"* (verse 5). This is one of many scriptures that teach the eternal security of the believer. If your name is ever recorded in the Book of Life, it will not be removed. *"Those that thou gavest me I have kept"* (John 17:12). No one can pluck us out of the Father's hand (John 10:29). We are secure because Jesus said so. It is not because of our works.

Conclusion: We learn from this text that the Lord always has a remnant, even in churches which appear to be dead.

The Church at Sardis had no persecution. Why would the devil waste his time on that which was lifeless? No church likes problems, but usually they are a sign that we are doing something to irritate our adversary.

"Philadelphia - The Church of the Open Door" (Revelation 3:7-13)

Introduction - This is one of the most refreshing churches. It is one of only two churches (the other was Smyrna) of whom the Lord found no fault. It was probably a small congregation, but they were faithful to the Word.

I. Open Door (Verses 7-9)

"And to the angel of the church in Philadelphia" (verse 7). The word "Philadelphia" means "brotherly love." This is an excellent name for the true followers of Jesus. *"By this shall all men know that ye are my disciples, if ye have love one to another"* (John 13:35). It would be good if all churches were known for their love.

The Lord Jesus has the "key of David." This is explained in Isaiah 22:22. King Hezekiah had a servant named Elikim. He was given a key to the palace called the *"key of David."* People had to go through Elikim to get to King Hezekiah. Likewise, the sinner must go through Christ to get to God. Jesus holds the key of hell and death (Revelation 1:18).

The Lord reminds us that He is able to open and close doors (verses 7 and 8). Our doors of service and ministry are controlled by the Father. If God opens a door for me, no man can close it. If the Lord closes a door of opportunity, we are wasting our time trying to get it open. After God closed the door to Noah's Ark, no one could get in (Genesis 7:16). If

God is calling you to some ministry, come now while the door is open.

The true believers would have authority over the *"synagogue of Satan"* (verse 9). These were false professors. They claimed to be God's people, but they were actually counterfeit church members. It pays to be on the winning side.

II. Awesome Deliverance (Verses 10 and 11)

A great promise is given to God's people in verse 10. *"Because thou hast kept the word of my patience, I also will keep thee from the hour of temptation, which shall come upon all the world, to try them that dwell upon the earth."*

The church at Philadelphia had honored the Word of God. Heaven and earth will pass away, but God's Word will not pass away (Matthew 24:35). *"Forever, O Lord, thy word is settled in Heaven"* (Psalm 119:89).

The *"hour of temptation"* appears to be a reference to the Tribulation. It would not refer to the normal trials of life because it will be a worldwide calamity. Only the Tribulation would seem to fit the description.

Conclusion: The overcomer is promised that he will become a *"pillar"* in the House of God (verse 12). A "pillar" speaks of stability. A child of God should be firmly planted in the roots of salvation. If we will stay in the Word, we will not be led astray by every false doctrine (Ephesians 4:14).

We are reminded anew of the importance of the Word of God. It will stand the test of time. If we will believe and stand upon that Word, it will see us through the storms of life.

"Laodicea - The Church Christ Could Not Enter"
(Revelation 3:14-22)

Introduction - The Church of Laodicea represents the end of the Church Age. It is the final and most disappointing of the churches. Laodicea is a picture of the modern church that has abandoned the preaching of the gospel.

I. The Lukewarm Church (Verses 14-17)

"And unto the angel of the church of the Laodiceans" (verse 14). The word "Laodicea" means "the rights of the people." This is an accurate definition of our current religious assemblies. People are running the church. God and His Will are ignored. You cannot please people and God at the same time. There is an old saying that has much truth--"Even Jesus Christ couldn't please folks at some of our churches."

Laodicea was a city that had many wealthy people living there. It appears from the text that affluence affected the outlook of the church.

It's quite interesting that the well-off church was doing the least spiritually. We are being bombarded in America with *"the prosperity gospel."* Jesus said it was easier for a camel to go through the eye of a needle than for a rich man to enter the kingdom of God (Matthew 19:24). This does not mean that God will not save a rich man. It is so easy for an individual to trust their riches rather than trust the Savior.

"The beginning of the creation of God" (verse 14). This description of Jesus has bothered many people. It does not mean that Jesus is the first thing created by God. That would make the Son inferior to the Father. A more accurate translation would be, "the beginner of the creation of God." The Lord Jesus is the ruler of God's creation. *"All things were made by Him"* (John 1:3). *"For by Him were all things created, that are in heaven, and that are in earth, visible and*

invisible...all things were created by Him, and for Him" (Colossians 1:16).

The most severe rebuke is given in verses 15 and 16. *"Thou art neither hot nor cold...because thou are lukewarm, and neither cold nor hot, I will spew thee out of my mouth."* There is an old saying, "When you straddle the fence, you will get shot at by both sides." The church at Laodicea would not take a stand one way or the other. What an accurate picture of the modern church.

Most church folks can be characterized as "lukewarm." We do just enough to keep the church going, but we don't want to get too involved. The world has no respect for half-hearted church members.

Luke-warmness even makes God sick. He said He would "spew" them out of His mouth. This means He will vomit them out.

We need to take a lesson from Joshua. *"Choose you this day whom ye will serve"* (Joshua 24:15). The time is approaching rapidly when we will be forced to choose sides in lukewarm America.

The Laodiceans were deceived about their spiritual condition. They thought they had need of nothing (verse 17). The church no doubt had beautiful facilities and money in the treasury.

Prosperity has just about killed the church in America. We have been blessed with fine buildings, a strong membership, and money in the bank. However, we are missing the old-time power of the Spirit of God. Our churches are well-organized, but anemic.

The Lord's evaluation of the church was that they were wretched, and miserable, and poor, and blind, and naked (verse 17). One can well imagine some feathers were ruffled when this letter was read aloud at the morning worship service.

II. The Loving Christ (Verses 18-22)

The Savior counsels the church to do several things

(verse 18). They were encouraged to "buy" that which is without money or price (Isaiah 55:1). They also were in desperate need of some spiritual eye-salve. Many of our churches need a few bottles of this today.

"As many as I love, I rebuke and chasten" (verse 19). This is a good way to tell if you are saved. Any person who can live in sin, enjoy it, and never be divinely disciplined has never been a child of God. Whom the Lord loves, He spanks when they get off track.

"Behold, I stand at the door, and knock: if any man hear my voice, and open the door, I will come in to him, and will sup with him, and he with me" (verse 20). This is the text that was used the night I made an open profession of faith in Christ. It is one of the favorite verses of evangelistic preachers. It is all right to do this, but if we take the verse in context, He is talking to the church.

The church had shut the Lord Jesus out. When I hear of the confusion in our modern churches, I realize that Jesus is nowhere around. Churches don't have to vote 100% on every matter, but they should love each other 100% of the time. Jesus is not in the midst of a divided church. The Lord is not the author of confusion (I Corinthians 14:33).

The overcomer is promised that he can sit with Jesus in His kingdom (verse 21). What a thrill that will be!

Conclusion: We learn from the church of Laodicea that riches and spirituality do not necessarily equate. The important thing is to be rich toward God.

"The Rapture of the Church" (Revelation 4 and 5)

Introduction - These chapters begin the third part of the book. Chapter One focused on the things which have been. Chapters Two and Three concerned the things which are or the Church Age. Now we will look at the things which are to come. I am grouping these two chapters together as they are concerned with the same material.

I. The Heavenly Throne (Verses 1-3)

"After this I looked, and, behold, a door was opened in Heaven" (verse 1). I believe this verse is telling us about the Rapture of the church. John begins by saying, *"After this."* After what? After the Church Age has culminated.

A door was opened in Heaven. John hears a trumpet sound. This corresponds perfectly with Rapture passages, such as I Corinthians 15:52 and I Thessalonians 4:16.

John was told to *"Come up hither"* (verse 1). The church is not mentioned again until a closing reference in Revelation 22:16. This is the major reason I do not believe the church will go through the Tribulation. The church is mentioned about 17 times in the first three chapters. Why would he suddenly stop talking about the church unless it was because it had been caught up to Heaven? The word "rapture" means "to snatch away" or to be "caught up."

"And immediately I was in the spirit" (verse 2). We will be taken to Heaven *"in the twinkling of an eye"* (I Corinthians 15:52). *"In the spirit"* indicates that John's spirit left his body so that he could be taken to Heaven. John's body could not go with him because it had not yet been glorified. No one can go to Heaven in an earthly body. That's why our bodies will be "changed" when the Lord comes (I Corinthians 15:51).

Before we look into Heaven, we need to understand something. When the Bible describes Heaven to individuals who have never been there, it uses symbols so that we can understand. For example, how could a person who lives in a primitive jungle go home and explain to his tribesmen such things as computers, televisions, or cell phones? It is just as difficult for us to understand heavenly things with earthly minds. Most of the symbols John used were connected to events in the Old Testament. None of us will fully understand the beauty of Heaven until we get there (I Corinthians 2:9).

"Behold, a throne was set in Heaven, and one sat on the throne" (verse 2). What will be the first thing we will look for when we get to Heaven? John's first observation is of a throne and One sitting on it. The One sitting on the throne is Jesus. John doesn't mention golden streets and pearly gates until much later (Revelation 21). Heaven will have to be a material place or there could be no throne.

This throne will be referred to at least 18 times in these two chapters. It will be the focal point of all that is happening.

John sees a rainbow around this throne (verse 3). The rainbow is a symbol of mercy. It was first mentioned in Genesis 9 when God promised to never again destroy the earth by a flood. The rainbow always appears after the storm is over. The storm will be over for the church.

There will be another throne mentioned in Chapter 20-- the Great White Throne. There will be no rainbow there. Every person will meet God at one of the thrones--with or without mercy. Those who are in Christ will be safe. *"There is, therefore, now no condemnation to them which are in Christ Jesus"* (Romans 8:1).

II. The 24 Elders (4:4-5)

Around the main throne, John sees 24 other thrones occupied by 24 elders (verse 4). Some speculate that these elders must be angels, but in the next chapter they speak of being redeemed (Revelation 5:9). Angels have never known redemption.

The most logical theory is that the elders consist of 12 representatives of the tribes of Israel and the 12 apostles. Can we find any other scripture where Israel and the apostles are seen together? In the description of the Heavenly City in Revelation 21, we discover 12 messengers at the gates and on the gates the names of the 12 tribes of the Children of Israel. The names of the 12 apostles are in the foundations of the city (Revelation 21:12-14).

These 24 elders will be wearing a crown of gold (verse 5). Crowns are symbols of reward for faithful service. They will not keep these crowns, but will place them at the precious feet of Jesus (verses 10-11). There is an implication of the Trinity here because the Third Person of the Godhead is described as a source of light. The Father and Son are also sources of light (Revelation 21:23). Therefore, we see that Father, Son, and Spirit are one.

III. The Living Creatures (4:6-9)

"Round about the throne, were four beasts full of eyes before and behind" (verse 6). A better interpretation of "beasts" here would be "living creatures." They represent the characteristics of God.

These "living creatures" are described in verses 7-9. It is important for us to note that these creatures are symbolic. There are not monsters in Heaven with faces of animals. These four creatures are obviously Cherubim, the highest order of angels. Lucifer was a Cherubim before he fell and became the devil (Ezekiel 28:14).

They gave praises to our God continually. *"They rest not day and night, saying, Holy, Holy, Holy, Lord God Almighty, which was, and is, and is to come"* (verse 8). Their praise will never end because God's glory will be eternal.

Perhaps we will join in and sing, *"All hail the power of Jesus' name, let angels prostrate fall, bring forth the royal diadem, and crown Him Lord of All."* The best is yet to come!

IV. The Seven-Sealed Book (Revelation 5:1-7)

When John's eyes had become more adjusted to Heaven, he began to notice what was happening. He notices a small scroll in the right hand of the One (God) sitting on the throne. It is very important that we identify the book because it is essential to understanding the rest of this prophecy.

This chapter is actually a continuation of Chapter Four. It begins with the conjunction "and" thus connecting the two chapters. This is why I have merged Chapters Four and Five.

"And I saw in the right hand of Him that sat on the throne a book...sealed with seven seals" (verse 1). At first, John sees no one but the Lord Jesus. He now observes another sitting on the same throne. This is obviously God the Father. We should not be confused about this because Father and Son are One (John 10:30).

The "book" was not a hard-bound book like we see so often. It was more like a scroll that was sealed with seven seals. We note again the number "seven" which is so prominent in Revelation. We have earlier studied the seven churches (chapters 2-3).

A strong angel then exclaims, *"Who is worthy to open the book?"* (verse 2). A search is then conducted to find someone adequate to break the seals and read the message. No mortal man was found to be worthy to open the book and read its contents (verse 3). It is a book of redemption and none of us are qualified to break its seals.

Everything now comes to a halt. John *"weeps much"* because none of the descendants of Adam can measure up to the absolute holiness that is required to be the Redeemer.

Many have been confused by the expression that John wept in Heaven. After all, aren't there supposed to be "no tears" up there? That teaching is based on a song and not scripture. The Word of God teaches that God will *"wipe away all tears"* (Revelation 21:4). How can He "wipe away" something that is not there? We need to distinguish between what songwriters say and what the Bible teaches.

The description of the scroll leads me to believe that it

contained the terms of redemption for this planet. Jesus redeemed our soul when He died at Calvary. He will redeem our body at the Rapture. He will redeem the earth and all creation during the opening of the seven seals. We must remember that all creation was affected by the Fall of Adam (Genesis 3:17-19).

This is why John became so emotional. He realized that everything depended upon finding a Redeemer. If the book could not be opened, all of creation would remain under the curse and the devil would continue to be victorious over this fallen real estate that we call "earth."

"And one of the elders saith unto me, "Weep not: behold, the Lion of the tribe of Judah, hath prevailed to open the book, and to loose the seven seals thereof" (verse 5). John can stop weeping because One is found who is capable of being our Redeemer. The Lord Jesus Christ is identified as *"the Lion of the tribe of Judah."* The Old Testament predicted long ago that the Messiah would come from the descendants of Judah (Genesis 49:10).

All earthly dignitaries have been disqualified because of sin. Only the Lord Jesus lived a perfect life and fulfilled all the requirement of a Holy God (I Peter 2:22). The word used in the Bible is "prevailed." It means to "overcome." He alone is worthy.

Jesus is both a *"Lion"* and a *"Lamb"* (verse 6). He will be as a Lion to those who reject His authority. He will appear as a sacrificial Lamb to those who love and trust Him.

We must not overlook the statement that the Lamb had been slain (verse 6). When we get to Heaven, we will never have any trouble recognizing Jesus. For all eternity, He will always carry the nail prints in His hands and feet. In addition, where His side was pierced will forever be visible. We will forever be reminded of the enormous price paid for our salvation. The marks in His body will be the only man-made things in Heaven.

"And He came and took the book out of the right hand of

Him that sat on the throne" (verse 7). What gave Him the right to do this? Because He went to the cross to pay our debt of sin and to liberate us from Satan's empire.

The earth is the Lord's because He created it. He leased it to Adam, but Adam forfeited it through sin. The Lord Jesus bought back what Adam lost when He hung on Calvary's tree.

Every person who has ever lived will either meet Him as a Lamb who died for their sins or as a Lion who will mete out judgment against them.

He is further identified as having *"seven horns and seven eyes, which are the seven Spirits of God"* (verse 6). Horns in scripture speak of power. He has all authority (Matthew 28:18). The "seven eyes" speak of the judicial power of the Lord Jesus, including the seven characteristics of the Holy Spirit that rest upon Him.

"He came and took the book" (verse 7). When the Lamb of God died on the cross, He redeemed the entire world to be His own. It was His by creation and now He has redeemed it for Himself. He sub-leased it to Adam, but Adam sub-leased it to the devil. Christ will return to this earth one day and everything will be made right.

V. "A New Song in Heaven" (Revelation 5:8-14)

This scripture informs us that a "pep rally" will take place in Heaven when the Lord Jesus begins to open the book of redemption. *"And they sung a new song"* (verse 9). There is no song recorded in the Book of Genesis. The first song in the Bible is found in Exodus 15. It was part of a praise celebration held after Almighty God had drowned the Egyptian soldiers in the Red Sea.

This song reminds us that Jesus is worthy to open the seven-sealed book. It is a "new song" because when we get to Heaven, all things will be new (Revelation 21:5). I hope the Lord will give me a new voice so that I can sing in a way that will honor Him.

Conclusion: The final verses of this chapter reveal to us that praise to the Lamb will go on forever (verses 11-14). The children of God will be on the winning side after all.

The apostle Paul tells us *"that at the name of Jesus every knee should bow"* (Philippians 2:10). We see the fulfillment of that in verse 13. Every creature will acknowledge that He is worthy. Even those who rejected Him will be forced to admit His authority.

Since you will one day admit that He is Lord, why not do it now? *"That if thou shalt confess with thy mouth the Lord Jesus, and shalt believe in thine heart that God hath raised Him from, the dead, thou shalt be saved"* (Romans 10:9).

"The Opening of the Seals" (Revelation 6:1-17)

Introduction - This chapter begins a series of fourteen chapters on the Tribulation Period. Although many Old Testament books describe this horrible time in some fashion, the Book of Revelation gives us the clearest perspective. Chapters six through nineteen focus on the seven-year period known as the Tribulation. Please note that the church is not mentioned during this critical time. If the Bride of Christ was still here, surely we would be told about it.

The Tribulation can be referred to by other names. It is also known in many Old Testament passages as the *"Day of the Lord"* (Zephaniah 1:14) or the "Time of Jacob's Trouble" (Jeremiah 30:7). Jacob's name was changed to Israel. The Tribulation will be a terrible time for everyone, but especially the Jews. Two-thirds of Abraham's descendants will perish under the atrocities of the Antichrist (Zechariah 13:8). After such misery, the Jews will gladly welcome the Messiah (Zechariah 12:10).

Jesus called this the most awful time ever seen on this planet (Matthew 24:21). It will begin with a seven-year peace agreement concerning Israel (Daniel 9:27). It will conclude with a worldwide conflict known as the War of Armageddon (Revelation 16:16).

Three distinct series of judgments will take place during this seven-year span of time. These include the seven seals, seven trumpets, and seven vials of wrath. If the Lord Jesus did not come back and stop the slaughter, man would annihilate himself (Matthew 24:22).

We shall begin by examining the seven seals.

I. The Four Horsemen (Revelation 6:1-8)

The first four seals deal with horsemen. We refer to them as the *"Four Horsemen of the Apocalypse"* (Revelation).

A. White Horse (Revelation 6:1-2)

"And I saw, and behold a white horse" (verse 2). Many have assumed that this rider is Christ since He will return riding a white horse (Revelation 19:11). We must be reminded here that the devil tries to counterfeit everything that God does.

The rider here is not Jesus Christ, but is rather the Antichrist. Our spiritual binoculars will reveal three major differences between this rider and the true Christ:

(1) The rider here appears at the beginning of the Tribulation. The Lord Jesus Christ will return at the end of the Tribulation.

(2) The rider here has a "bow", but no arrow. This means he will appear initially to be a man of peace because the arrow is the deadly part of the bow and arrow. *"By peace shall destroy many"* (Daniel 8:25). By contrast, the only weapon Jesus will have is the power of His Word. *"And out of His mouth goeth a sharp sword"* (Revelation 19:15). The Word of God will defeat the devil and his followers.

(3) The rider here has a *"crown"* and Jesus will wear *"many crowns"* (Revelation 19:12). There are two different Greek words that are translated as "crown". The rider in Chapter Six is wearing a crown translated from the Greek word "Stephanos." It means an artificial crown. The word translated as "crown" in Revelation 19:12 is "diadem." It means He will have all authority and power.

B. Red Horse (Revelation 6:3,4)

"And there went out another horse that was red" (verse 4). The "red horse" stands for bloodshed and warfare. Thus, we see that the Antichrist's peace process won't last long.

"There was given unto him a great sword." He will have the ability to stir up hatred among various groups of people. We are living in a world that is becoming more dangerous with each passing day. Life is not valued at all by the majority of mankind.

We will always have evil people and leaders. There will be no lasting peace until the return of the Prince of Peace. Man has sophisticated weaponry today, but his heart is still corrupt.

The spirit of "Antichrist" will so inflame men that there will be class wars, racial wars, ethnic wars, etc. Praise God for the day when men will *"beat their swords into plow-shares, and their spears into pruning hooks"* (Isaiah 2:4).

C. Black Horse (Revelation 6:5,6)

"And I beheld and lo a black horse" (verse 5). As the third seal is opened, we observe a black horse and its rider. This represents worldwide famine. Famine usually follows major wars. Farm land will be rendered useless by mass weapons of destruction.

"He that sat on him had a pair of balances in his hand." Balances represent scarcity. Wheat and barley will have to be rationed. A "measure" of wheat and barley are mentioned in verse six. A "measure" is enough food for one person for one day. What if he has a family? A man will have to work all day for a "penny". This is not one cent as we think of a penny. The Greek word "denarius" means "a day's wage". The time will soon come when people would rather have food than money. Decisions will have to be made about who will eat and who will not.

The rider is instructed not to hurt the oil and wine. These are the traditional foods of the rich. It means there will only be two classes of people during the Tribulation--the very rich and the very poor. There will be no middle class.

D. Pale Horse (Revelation 6:7,8).

The opening of the fourth seal introduces us to the most fearsome rider of all.

"And I looked, and behold a pale horse" (verse 8). The word "pale" is the Greek word "chloros". It means a "pale green". The "pale horse" stands for disease and pestilence. A pestilence is a disease that has become an epidemic.

Scientists are currently talking about a coming pandemic that will take the lives of millions. This verse teaches that disease will claim one-fourth of the world's population. A later prophecy explains that warfare will claim one-third of the earth's inhabitants (Revelation 9:18). If we combine these two verses, we will learn that approximately one-half of the earth's residents will perish during the seven years of the Tribulation. No wonder that Jesus called it the worse time even seen in this world (Matthew 24:21).

"Death and hell" will ride on this horse. Death claims the body and Hell (Hades) claims the soul of the unsaved.

The Lord Jesus gave an interesting parallel passage to the Four Horsemen in Matthew 24:1-7. Jesus is asked by his disciples, *"When shall these things be? and what shall be the sign of thy coming, and of the end of the world?"* (Matthew 24:3). Jesus proceeded to tell them about the signs of the end and in doing so, He predicted the arrival of the four riders.

Religious deceivers are mentioned in Matthew 24:5. This stands for the rider on the white horse. *"And ye shall hear of wars and rumours of wars"* (Matthew 24:6). This is the red horse. Our Savior predicted famines and pestilences in Matthew 24:7. Famines would stand for the black horse and pestilences would describe the pale horse.

Jesus not only referenced the Four Horsemen, but He listed them in the order they appear in Revelation.

II. Restless Martyrs (Revelation 6:9-11)

The imagery changes with the opening of the fifth seal. The final three seals have no connection with horsemen.

"And when he had opened the fifth seal, I saw under the altar the souls of them that were slain for the word of God, and for the testimony which they held" (verse 9). We must identify these martyred saints. These are they who refused to follow the Antichrist and were put to death as a result. Most of these will probably be Jewish. Most Jews are currently in spiritual blindness (Romans 11:25). After the church is raptured, many of them will come to repentance.

They cry out for God to bring justice on their persecutors (verse 10). Please observe that these souls are conscious and aware of what is happening. The Word of God does not teach soul-sleep. Sleep only refers to the body and never to the soul.

We learn from this scripture that the dead are aware of earthly events. They may not know everything, but they have knowledge of major events. For example, Jesus said there would be rejoicing in Heaven when someone repents (Luke 15:7). How could they be excited if they didn't know about it?

The Lord assures them that He will bring retribution in due time (verse 11). He tells them to be patient. I think we need this advice as well. The hour of judgment is fixed. We can take comfort to know that our Father is still in control.

We will meet these believers again in Revelation 20:4 where they will live and reign with Christ for a thousand years.

III. World's Last Prayer Meeting (Revelation 6:12-17). The sixth seal finds the earth going into convulsions. Some have read this and speculated that a nuclear explosion had taken place.

I believe the passage should be taken both symbolically and literally. Symbolically, all society is falling apart and people are perplexed. Literally, there will be a shaking of this tired planet.

"There was a great earthquake ... sun became black ... moon became as blood" (verse 12). Stars will fall unto the earth and mountains and islands will roll around as basket-balls (verses 13 and 14).

A final prayer meeting will be called in response to these frightening events (verses 15-17). All elements of society will be present. Their prayer is recorded in verse 16. *"And said to the mountains and rocks, Fall on us, and hide us from the face of him that sitteth on the throne, and from the wrath of the Lamb."*

Pity the prosperity preachers in this day of God's judgment. God will finally get the attention of rebellious men.

The sad thing is they prayed to the mountains and rocks. Their only motive was to escape the Lord's wrath. They prayed to the rocks when they could have prayed to the Rock of Ages. They desired to be hidden <u>from</u> God when they could have been hidden <u>in</u> Him.

Conclusion: Prayer meetings today are often ignored. People have other things to do. However, this service will attract a large number of folks.

These awesome events will not lead to repentance and revival. Despite the attitude of some religious folks, it is the goodness of God that leads to repentance (Romans 2:4).

"The 144,000" (Revelation 7:1-17)

Introduction - We have observed the opening of the six seals. This chapter features a pause before the final seal is opened.

Have you ever wondered if people would be saved during the Tribulation? Who will be doing the preaching if the church has been taken away? This chapter reveals the answer. Never forget that God will always have a remnant to represent Him.

I. Preachers (verses 1-8)

God is going to seal 144,000 servants so that they might proclaim His Word during these dark hours of Tribulation (verses 3-4). They will be sealed in their foreheads. This will apparently be some type of visible mark. During the current Age of Grace, every true believer is sealed with the Holy Spirit (Ephesians 4:30).

The devil attempts to copy or counterfeit everything that is done by God. Our adversary will also require that a seal be placed upon his followers (Revelation 13:16). The Satanic seal is better known as the Mark of the Beast.

This passage of scripture has been one of the most misunderstood and misinterpreted portions of Holy Scripture. All kinds of cults have claimed to be the fulfillment of this text.

The Bible itself reveals the identity of these evangelists. There were 12,000 from each of the twelve tribes of the *"children of Israel"* (verse 4). In other words, every one of them is a Jew. God is going to return to working through the nation of Israel.

The twelve tribes are identified in verses 5-8. There is no such thing as the "ten lost tribes." They may have been scattered, but the Lord knows where they are. Don't you know that if God lost track of some of the Jews, He may forget where we are. This is a divine impossibility.

Will the 144,000 evangelists have any success?

II. Results (verses 9-17)

"After this I beheld, and, lo, a great multitude, which no man could number, of all nations, and kindreds, and people, and tongues, stood before the throne" (verse 9). Some have mistakenly identified this multitude as the raptured church.

The group is clearly identified in verse 14. *"These are they which came out of great tribulation."* They are wearing white robes (purity) and have palms in their hands (victory). This great number of people prove that the 144,000 will be successful. Their converts will come from all areas of the earth.

They will have suffered greatly under the government of the Antichrist. They will never again know hunger nor thirst because the Lamb will see to it that every need is satisfied (verses 16 and 17). They may not have been able to purchase earthly provisions, but God will feed them with heavenly manna.

God will personally wipe away all tears from their eyes (verse 17). This same promise is later made to all the other believers (Revelation 21:4).

Conclusion: This chapter is important because it answers some frequently asked questions. Who will carry out the preaching after the church is gone? The answer is the 144,000 Jews who have been called and sealed. Can people be saved during the Tribulation? The answer is there will be a great multitude who will believe the testimony of the Jewish witnesses.

Since there will be people saved during the Tribulation, we need to answer the question of whether or not God will give individuals a "second chance." The Apostle Paul clarifies that in II Thessalonians 2:10-12. Those people who are living today and have the truth of the gospel and reject it will not have another opportunity to be saved. God will send them a delusion and harden their hearts. They will believe a lie because they rejected the truth and the Truth is Jesus (John 14:6).

If God gave these people a "second chance", He would have to resurrect all other lost people and give them another opportunity to be saved.

The *"great multitude"* here represents those who had never heard the gospel or had not been given an opportunity to accept or reject Christ. If you hear His voice, respond to-day while you may (II Corinthians 6:2).

"The Seven Trumpets" (Revelation 8 and 9)

Introduction - Once again, I am combining these two chapters, as I did earlier with Chapters 4 and 5. Six trumpets will sound during these two chapters as God begins to bring more severe judgments on this wicked world.

The seven trumpets actually fall under the seventh seal (verse 1). We had studied the first six seals in Chapter 6.

Seven angels are seen standing before the Lord (verse 2). They were given seven trumpets to blow. At the sound of each trumpet a judgment was poured out on the earth. Bible students will connect the seven trumpets with the fall of Jericho (Joshua 6). Jericho fell when the seven trumpets were blown. This world will also collapse at the coming of God's wrath.

Only six of the trumpets will be identified in these two chapters. There will be another divine time-out. The seventh trumpet will be sounded in Revelation 11:15, *"The kingdoms of this world are become the kingdoms of our Lord, and of his Christ; and he shall reign for ever and ever."*

Let's now take a look at the seven trumpets.

I. First Trumpet (8:7)

"The first angel sounded, and there followed hail and fire mingled with blood, and they were cast upon the earth: and the third part of trees was burnt up, and all green grass was burnt up."

Many of these trumpet judgments were similar to the plagues on Egypt as found in the book of Exodus. The Lord sent hail and fire during the seventh plague on Pharaoh (Exodus 9:18-26).

There is an element of mercy mingled with this divine judgment. Only the third part of the trees were destroyed. Two-thirds were spared. The expression, "one-third" will appear frequently in these two chapters.

II. Second Trumpet (verses 8 and 9)

"And the second angel sounded, and as it were a great mountain burning with fire was cast into the sea...third part...became blood...third part...creatures...died...third part of the ships were destroyed."

Please note that the Bible did not say that it was a literal mountain, but "as it were" or "like" a mountain. It was likely a giant meteorite. The result of the death and the chemical make-up of the meteorite turns the water into blood. The Lord turned the Nile River into blood as the initial plague upon Egypt (Exodus 7:19-20).

When the Bible refers to "sea", it usually means the Mediterranean. This sea is currently the western boundary of Israel. There will no doubt be many ships in these waters as the world increasingly focuses on the Middle East.

III. Third Trumpet (8:10-11)

"And the third angel sounded, and there fell a great star from heaven, burning as it were a lamp...name of the star is called Wormwood...waters...were made bitter."

Once again, we must state that this was not a literal lamp that fell out of the sky, but "as it were" a lamp. It was burning like a huge lamp. This will probably be some type of meteorite. One-third of the rivers and fountains of water will be poisoned by the gasses from this flaming torch. The waters will be made very bitter.

This falling star has a name. It is called Wormwood (verse 11). Wormwood is a bitter, intoxicating, poisonous herb. It has the ability to paralyze and kill its victims. In the Old Testament, God threatened to send wormwood upon His disobedient people (Jeremiah 9:15). This may be because His enemies gave Jesus bitter gall at Calvary. They will reap what they've sown.

IV. Fourth Trumpet (8:12-13)

"And the fourth angel sounded ... third part of the sun was smitten ... third part of the moon ... third part of the stars ... darkened."

This trumpet deals with luminous bodies--sun, moon, and stars. The Lord made these bodies on the fourth day and He darkens them as a result of the fourth trumpet. If God could create light, He would certainly be able to reduce it by one-third.

The judgments will intensify. An angel flies through the heavens declaring, *"Woe, woe, woe to the inhabiters of the earth"* (verse 13). The three "woes" stand for the fifth, sixth, and seventh trumpet judgments.

The Lord Jesus spoke of this dreadful time when He said, *"And there shall be signs in the sun, and in the moon, and in the stars...Men's hearts failing them for fear"* (Luke 21:25,26). God is about to send a shaking the likes of which has never before been seen in this world.

Natural disasters should intensify if we are truly living in the last days before our Lord's return.

V. Fifth Trumpet (9:1-2)

"And the fifth angel sounded, and I saw a star fall from heaven unto the earth: and to him was given the key of the bottomless pit" (verse 1).

This verse has created a good bit of disagreement among Bible students. Some believe the "star" referred to here is the devil. Others believe that it is Jesus. Isn't it interesting that the answers can be so completely opposite of one another.

There are several important things about this verse that we must consider. "Star" is in the past tense. A more accurate translation would be "a star fallen from heaven". It refers to an event that had happened sometime in the past. Jesus spoke of this when He said, *"I beheld Satan as lightning fall from heaven"* (Luke 10:18).

The devil was originally Lucifer, the most beautiful of all the angels. Information regarding his fall is given in Isaiah 14 and Ezekiel 28.

It is obvious this "star" is a person because *"to _him_ was given the key of the bottomless pit."*

In the Greek manuscripts, the "bottomless pit" is the

word "abyss." Reference to the "abyss" is found nine times in the New Testament and more than thirty times in the Old Testament.

The "bottomless pit" or the "abyss" contains some of the worst demons or fallen angels who followed Lucifer in his rebellion against Almighty God. A study of scripture reveals two kinds of demons. Some are free and roam about seeking to indwell men and others are locked up in the "bottomless pit". The Apostle Peter refers to these evil spirits when he writes about the angels that sinned and have been bound "into chains of darkness" (II Peter 2:4). If things are bad now in this old world, what will it be like when the worst demons are turned loose?

The loosing of these wicked creatures is the focus of both the fifth and sixth trumpets. The prophet Joel describes this time as well (Joel 2:1-11).

When the "bottomless pit" is opened, demon locusts appear to torment men. The Bible gives us a couple of clues to let us know that these "locusts" are not literal insects. The locust plague in Exodus 10:15 stripped every green thing in the land of Egypt. However, these "locusts" are commanded not to harm the vegetation nor those with the seal of God. This reassures us that God is still in control.

The main reason we know these "locusts" are not insects is given in verse 11. *"And they had a king over them."* Locusts have no king (Proverbs 30:27). This "king" is given two names--Abaddon and Apollyon. Both names mean "destroyer" This "king" is the destroyer of souls--obviously, it is the devil.

The activity of these "demon locusts" is revealed in verses 5 through 10. They will torment men for five months. During this period of time, things will be so miserable that men will try to kill themselves, but will be unable to do so (verse 6). The torment of the ungodly is just beginning.

VI. Sixth Trumpet (Revelation 9:13-21)

"And the sixth angel sounded...Loose the four angels which

are bound in the great river Euphrates" (verses 13-14). We could entitle this section, "Angels at the River", but we must remember these are evil angels. It is obvious that they are wicked because they are restrained.

Please note they were bound near the Euphrates River. This is in the area where the Garden of Eden was located. It makes me believe that these four wicked angels had something to do with the fall of Adam. They were so vile that God locked them up. In this time of Tribulation, they will be released to torture man.

The Euphrates River is mentioned twice in the Revelation--here and in Revelation 16:12. The Nile River and the Euphrates formed the boundaries of the Promised Land.

Once again, God carefully controls the exact time that these demons will have to be free. They will create havoc for one year, one month, one day, and one hour (verse 15). They will stir up such hatred that one-third of the earth's population will be killed during this interval. In Revelation 6:8, we saw where one-fourth were killed. If we put these two verses together, we learn that approximately one-half of the earth's population will die during the seven years of the Tribulation.

These four loosed angels will entice an army of *"two hundred thousand thousand"* (verse 16). This is an army of 200 million. It is not clear from the text if this refers to men or demons. This army will be riding upon horse-like creatures, with heads like lions, and giving off fire, smoke, and brimstone. They have tails like serpents, from which their power is sent out (verses 17-19). This could very well be a preview of the carnage at Armageddon. The world is currently moving toward this end-time conflict at a rapid pace.

Conclusion: Wouldn't you think by this time that people would be anxious to repent? The closing verses in this chapter reveal that men's hearts become more hardened instead (verses 20-21). Generally speaking, misery and suffering do not lead to repentance. Rather, it is the goodness of God that draws a lost sinner (Romans 2:4).

Men cannot be saved on their own timetable, but on God's. God's time is today (II Corinthians 6:2).

"The Angel and the Book" (Revelation 10:1-11)

Introduction - This chapter is a pause between the sixth and seventh trumpets. There was a similar pause between the sixth and seventh seals.

The Lord will be preparing the Apostle John for the work remaining in this great prophecy.

The chapter focuses on a mighty angel and a little book. The identity of both has caused much speculation throughout the centuries.

An interesting sidelight is found in verse 4. Seven thunders give forth a message, but John was forbidden to write those things down. Once again, this had led to much speculation, but we just don't know what the thunders said.

I. The Angel

"And I saw another mighty angel come down from heaven, clothed with a cloud: and a rainbow was upon his head, and his face was as it were the sun, and his feet as pillars of fire:" (verse 1). Most Bible scholars believe that the "mighty angel" is actually the Lord Jesus Christ. The description given here is practically identical to that of Christ in Revelation 1:15-16.

When He appeared in the Old Testament, Jesus was referred to as "the Angel of the Lord. He appeared in this form to the Jews. Since most of the remaining part of Revelation will involve Israel, it makes sense that Jesus will reveal Himself as a mighty angel.

Israel's blindness will be lifted when He descends from

Heaven and they observe the wounds He suffered for their redemption. They will mourn as one that is grieving for his firstborn son (Zechariah 12:10).

II. The Book

"And he had in his hand a little book open:" (verse 2). Bible students are divided as to the identity of the "little book". I am not dogmatic here, but the "little book" seems to be the same book mentioned in Chapter 5. Since the seals have been broken and we know what they are, it is possible that the book is no longer needed; therefore, John is told to eat it. (verse 9).

Another suggestion that sounds reasonable is that the "little book" contains the events from this point on until the end of the Book of Revelation.

John is told to take the *"little book"* from the *"mighty angel"* and *"eat it up"* (verse 9). The book was as *"sweet as honey"* in his mouth but it became bitter in his stomach (verse 10). This illustrates that the Word of God is a two-edged sword (Hebrews 4:12). It is both sweet and bitter at the same time. It is sweet to the believer because it promises us eternal life with our Savior. However, it is bitter to the unbeliever because it warns of Hell to the lost.

Conclusion: Every God-called preacher has an obligation to preach the truth and not just tickle the ears of unbelievers. Our job is not to make the message popular, but to make it clear.

A preacher, who balances his sermons between God's love and His justice is truly preaching the full gospel. Believe on the Lord Jesus Christ and you will be saved (Acts 16:31). Reject the message and the wrath of God abides on you (John 3:36).

"The Two Witnesses" (Revelation 11:1-14)

Introduction - The first part of this chapter continues the pause between the sixth and seventh trumpet judgments.

This chapter describes the ministry of two men who will have an enormous impact during the Tribulation. Their identity has been the subject of much debate by Bible students.

John is told to *"Rise and measure the temple of God"* (verse 1). From this verse, we know that the Jewish temple will be rebuilt after the Rapture of the church. This will be the third temple for the Jews. The first one was destroyed by the Babylonians under Nebuchadnezzar. The second temple was demolished in 70 A.D. by the Romans.

There is much talk in Israel today about preparations for a third temple. Surely this must mean we are living in the end times. The only reason for the delay in constructing this end-time place of worship is the fact that the Muslims have built a structure on the exact spot where the first temples stood. It is called the Dome of the Rock or the Mosque of Omar. Thus, we see that the Temple Mount area in Jerusalem is holy to the descendants of both Isaac and Ishmael. Politicians today fail to understand that the conflict in the Middle East is religious, not political.

Will the Lord have someone to speak on His behalf in Jerusalem?

I. The Two Witnesses (Revelation 11:3-13)

  A. Ministry (verses 3-6)

"And I will give power unto my two witnesses" (verse 3). These two individuals will have a ministry of 1260 days or 3 1/2 years. They will prophecy during the first half of the Tribulation. Their message will be one of judgment. That is why they will be wearing sackcloth.

They are referred to as *"olive trees"* (verse 4). This relates back to an Old Testament passage in Zechariah 4:3. It literally means "trees of oil". Oil is symbolic of the Holy Spirit; therefore, we know the Holy Spirit will empower these two men.

Bible scholars have been fascinated as to the identity of these special witnesses. Many believe they are Enoch and Elijah because those two left here without passing through the Valley of Death. Some conclude that they must come back and die because *"it is appointed unto men once to die"* (Hebrews 9:27). That verse, however, does not necessarily refer to all men individually but rather to mankind as a whole. For example, there is going to be one generation of believers who will leave here without checking in at the funeral home (I Corinthians 15:51).

Elijah does indeed seem to fit the description of one of the witnesses. The Old Testament closes by predicting his return before the *"great and dreadful day of the Lord"* (Malachi 4:5,6).

The powers associated with Elijah are highlighted in verses 5 and 6. This witness will be able to use fire to devour his enemies. Elijah is the *"prophet of fire"* (I Kings 18:24-38). These men will have authority to shut up heaven that it will not rain for 3 1/2 years (verse 6). Elijah prayed and no rain fell in Israel for 3 1/2 years (James 5:17). It appears obvious that Elijah will be one of the witnesses.

The debate centers around the second witness. I do not believe that it was Enoch. He was a Gentile who lived hundreds of years before Abraham. Enoch is not identified with Israel in any way. He is actually a type or picture of the New Testament church which will be raptured or taken out before the flood of judgment erupts on this poor world.

It makes sense to me that the second witness will be Moses. This is based on what the witnesses will be able to do. Two things in the sixth verse lead me to believe that Moses will be the second witness. They *"have power over waters to turn them to blood."* The first plague on Egypt involved waters being turned to blood (Exodus 7:17). The witnesses will also be able *"to smite the earth with all plagues."* Moses was instrumental in the ten plagues being brought upon Egypt as recorded in Exodus 7 to Exodus 12.

We must ask the question, is there any place in scripture where Moses and Elijah appear together? These two came down from heaven together to speak with Jesus on the Mount of Transfiguration (Matthew 17:1-5).

It is also interesting to consider what happened to the bodies of Moses and Elijah. Elijah never died. His body was transformed or raptured as he was taken up by a whirlwind and a chariot of fire (II Kings 2:11). The Lord Himself took the body of Moses and buried it. No man ever knew where he was buried (Deuteronomy 3:4-6). The archangel Michael fought with Satan over the body of Moses (Jude 9).

B. Persecution (verses 7-10)

These two supernatural agents will be put to death by the beast after they "have finished their testimony" (verse 7). We will study the beast in detail in Chapter 13. He will be unable to kill these servants of God until their work is done. If we are in God's will, the devil cannot have us put to death prematurely.

Their enemies will leave their bodies to lie in the streets of Jerusalem for 3 1/2 days (verses 8 and 9). The whole world will witness this event. This would have been impossible before the development of satellites and television.

"And they that dwell upon the earth shall rejoice over them, and make merry, and shall send gifts one to another" (verse 10). Sadly, some Biblically ignorant people have used this verse on Christmas Cards. This is the devil's crowd that is rejoicing because God's spokesmen have apparently been silenced.

C. Resurrection (verses 11-14)

"The Spirit of Life from God entered into them, and they stood upon their feet; and great fear fell upon them which saw them" (verse 11). God will supernaturally resurrect their dead bodies after 3 1/2 days have elapsed.

God then calls them up to heaven with the words *"Come up hither"* (verse 12). This is identical to the invitation John received in Revelation 4:1.

A great earthquake will then level one-tenth of the city of Jerusalem (verse 13). Seven thousand people will die at that chaotic time. Major news outlets will no doubt have plenty to report to their viewers.

II. The Seventh Trumpet (verses 15-19)

The seventh trumpet of judgment finally sounds. We studied the first six trumpets in Chapters 8 and 9. A glorious announcement is made. *"The kingdoms of this world are become the kingdoms of our Lord, and of His Christ; and He shall reign for ever and ever"* (verse 15). The language in this verse is written as though it had already happened. Actually, the change of authority will not occur until Chapter 19.

Conclusion: We note in closing that *"the temple of God was opened in heaven"* (verse 19). Did you know that there is a literal temple in heaven? The Tabernacle and Temples of the Old Testament were copies of the one in heaven (Exodus 25:40 and Hebrews 9:23).

The fact that John saw the temple of God and the ark indicates that Israel is coming into view and that God will resume His dealings with that nation. Judgment is coming, but God will preserve His own.

"The Rise of Anti-Semitism" (Revelation 12:1-17)

Introduction - One of the most tragic facts of history is the continuing irrational hatred and persecution of the Jewish people. Since they are descendants of Shem, they can be referred to as Semitic people. Anti-Semitism is a violent hatred of God's chosen people with a desire to see them exterminated.

This philosophy of Anti-Semitism has existed throughout history. The very fact that the Jews have survived as a distinct people is a testimony to the faithfulness of God.

When you meet an individual who hates the Jews, you can "take it to the bank" that Satan is motivating that person. It is an irrational hatred because the Jews make up less than one-fourth of one percent of the world's population. How could they be responsible for all of the world's problems?

As terrible as Anti-Semitism has been in the past, it will reach its boiling point during the Tribulation. The devil will be expelled from heaven completely and will find lodging in a world leader known as the Antichrist or the Beast. Persecution of Israel will intensify greatly under this satanic leader.

This chapter is also known as the "sign" chapter. The word "wonder" in the text means "sign". A proper understanding of this chapter will help us to know what will happen to Israel when all other nations have turned their backs on her.

I. The Woman and the Dragon (Verses 1-6)

We are immediately introduced to a very unusual woman. She is wearing the sun for a dress; the moon for her shoes; and a crown with twelve stars for her hat. She is pregnant and her delivery is at hand (verses 1 and 2).

Who is the peculiar woman and what does this mean? Is there any other place in scripture where we have the sun, moon, and twelve stars brought together in a similar way?

We may refer back to Joseph's dream (Genesis 37:9). He beheld the sun, moon, and eleven stars being made subject unto him. Joseph himself was the twelfth star. His father, Jacob, saw in this a picture of the nation of Israel with its twelve tribes.

Therefore, we conclude that the woman stands for the nation of Israel. We are to understand that the Lord is not through with the Jewish people. Israel has temporarily been set aside as God works with the church, but the day is coming when Israel will once again be the focus of God's program for the nations.

The woman was *"with child"* and experiencing the labor of birth pains (verse 2). All through the Old Testament the Jews had anticipated the coming of the Messiah. He was first promised on the day when Adam and Eve sinned (Genesis 3:15).

As soon as the promise of the Child was given there appeared a dragon who attempted to destroy the Child. Who is the dragon? This one is easy because verse 9 identifies him as Satan or the devil. He is pictured here as having seven heads and ten horns and seven crowns upon his heads. We will discuss this in Chapter 13.

"And his tail drew the third part of the stars of heaven" Verse 4). The "stars" mentioned here are angels. Lucifer or Satan was at one time the leader of the stars (Isaiah 14:12). Lucifer means "son of the morning" or "the morning star". He became jealous of Jehovah God and persuaded one-third of the angels to join him in a revolt.

These rebellious creatures fell from their place of shining. Some of the worst ones are reserved in chains of darkness (Jude 6). These fallen angels are also referred to as evil spirits, demons, and devils. There is only one devil, but there are many demons.

The dragon was ready to destroy the woman's child as soon as it was born (verse 4). In Genesis 3:15, God announced that the Seed of the Woman would bruise the serpent's head. At that time, war was declared between the devil and Jesus, the Seed of the Woman. Bible students refer to it as *"the conflict of the ages."*

Satan was poised to destroy baby Jesus immediately after He was born. The evil one put it into the mind of King Herod to have all male babies around Bethlehem to be slaughtered (Matthew 2:16).

The woman's child will *"rule all nations with a rod of iron"* (verse 5). This is a reference to the rule of Christ in the millennial kingdom. It is predicted in Psalm 2:9.

Further identification is given when *"her child was caught up unto God."* This is an obvious reference to the resurrection of our Savior. He was caught up to Heaven and is now seated at the right hand of God. We saw Him on His throne in Revelation 4 and 5.

"And the woman fled into the wilderness" (verse 6). Please observe that when the Child was taken to Heaven, the woman fled. The Jews were scattered as a people shortly after Jesus went back to be with the Father.

The 1,260 days or 3 1/2 years of the Tribulation are mentioned again. During this awful time, the Jews will need a hiding place from the anger of the Antichrist. God took care of His people in the wilderness during the time of the Exodus and He will do so again. The devil will never succeed in destroying all of God's children.

II. War in Heaven (Verses 7-12)

While wars will be fought on earth during the Tribulation, we discover in this passage that war will also break out in the heavens. The devil and his angels will make an effort to take control of the universe from Almighty God.

We are introduced to Michael, the greatest of the angels (verse 7). He is referred to as an archangel in Jude 9. He will stand up for the Jews during the Tribulation and will keep them from being destroyed (Daniel 12:1). His name means "one like God". He was probably promoted to his rank as the most powerful angel after the fall of Lucifer.

Despite his power, Michael does not seem to be able to cope with Satan, one-on-one, but must rely on the power of God. This is an excellent lesson for believers. If the archangel Michael is not strong enough to take on Satan, neither are we. This is why we must put on the whole armor of God (Ephesians 6:11).

The result of the heavenly conflict is already settled. The devil *"prevailed not"* (verse 8), but *"was cast out into the earth"* (verse 9). If you think things are bad now, just wait until the devil is thrown to the earth. I believe that it will be at that time he will enter into the body of an individual known as the Antichrist or Beast (Revelation 13).

This might be a good place to summarize Satan's travel agenda. God did not create the devil. He created Lucifer, a beautiful angel, who was the *"anointed cherub"* (Ezekiel 28:14). He was apparently the most beautiful and intelligent of all the heavenly creatures.

Lucifer led a revolt against God and was cast out of Heaven (Isaiah 14:12). He is currently the *"prince of the power of the air"* (Ephesians 2:2). He will be cast to the earth according to Revelation 12:9. From the earth, he will be sent to the *"bottomless pit"* (Revelation 20:3). His final destination will be the *"lake of fire"* (Revelation 20:10).

Thus, we see that Satan's best days are behind him. When he reminds you of your past, remind him of his future. It is all downhill.

Four names are used for our adversary in this verse-- dragon, serpent, Devil, and Satan. There can be no identity theft here.

Three weapons are listed in verse 11 for the believer in his spiritual conflict with the evil one. First is the "blood of the Lamb." There is power in the blood of Jesus. The blood is a symbol that Satan is a defeated foe. If he tried to go through the blood to get to us, he would become a saved devil. Our second weapon is the *"word of their testimony."* The redeemed of the Lord need to speak up (Psalm 107:2).

Many may remember the old-fashioned testimony meetings. Our third source of strength is *"they loved not their lives unto the death."* Our spiritual life is more important than the physical. *"And fear not them which kill the body...but rather fear Him which is able to destroy both soul and body in hell"* (Matthew 10:28).

Heaven rejoices when the devil is cast out, but earth can only expect more trouble (verse 12). Satan will intensify his efforts as he knows that his time is running out.

III. Preservation of the Jews (Verses 13-17)

The devil will focus his main artillery against the Jews (verse 13). A final holocaust will be instigated. Two-thirds of the Jews will perish (Zechariah 13:8).

God will supernaturally protect a Jewish remnant (verse 14). An eagle is mentioned as the source of Israel's deliverance. This is **not** a reference to the United States. It refers back to the time of Israel's deliverance from Pharaoh (Exodus 19:4). As He miraculously delivered His ancient people, He will also spare a remnant of Israel in the future.

Israel will be provided *"for a time, and times, and half a time."* This is 3 1/2 years or the last half of the Tribulation.

The closing verses of the chapter indicate a continuing conflict between the serpent and the woman. The serpent unleashes some type of flood upon the woman (verse 15), but the earth will swallow it up (verse 16). This will infuriate the devil so that he steps up his attack on the remnant of people who have the testimony of Jesus Christ (verse 17).

Conclusion: As the world moves steadily away from Israel, one thing is abundantly clear. God will preserve the descendants of Abraham. Though all nations forsake her, Almighty God will not. One of the sure signs of the coming of the Lord is the growing international opposition to the state of Israel.

The enemies of Israel are formidable. However, God has promised that there will always be a Jew (Jeremiah 31:35

"The Two Beasts" (Revelation 13:1-18)

Introduction - As we saw in the preceding chapter, the devil has been cast down to the earth. He will literally take possession of a world leader known as the Beast or Antichrist. This satanic superman will have a charismatic helper known as the Second Beast or False Prophet (Revelation 19:20). These Two Beasts, along with Satan himself, make up the Satanic Trinity.

The stage is being set for the arrival of the Antichrist. The world is looking for a leader who will have all the answers. The Bible refers to him as a beast, but the world will be ready to worship him (Revelation 13:4).

Let's look carefully at these two men who will deceive the world into following them to Armageddon.

I. The First Beast (Revelation 13:1-10)

"Beast rise up out of the sea...seven heads and ten horns" (verse 1). The Beast is simply another name for the Antichrist. Actually, he has several names in scripture--the little horn, the king of fierce countenance, the prince that shall come, the Abomination of Desolation, the son of perdition, the man of sin, the lawless one, etc. The Bible calls him a "beast" because of his horrible ways.

The "sea" in scripture refers to nations in turmoil. Therefore, we are to understand that the Antichrist will emerge during a time of international confusion. The world today is ready to follow any leader that will give unity and peace.

Major problems are now global in scope. Terrorism, global warming, and economic difficulties will only be solved by nations working together. Sadly, these problems will lead to the rise of a world dictator.

The "seven heads" apparently refers to Rome, the city built on seven hills (Revelation 17:9). The old Roman Empire will be re-united under ten kingdoms or blocs of nations (Daniel 7:24; Revelation 17:12). This explains the "ten horns" of the beast.

For over 1500 years, men have struggled to put the old Roman Empire back together. Charlemagne, Napoleon, and Mussolini all failed in this effort. Only the Antichrist will be able to pull it off.

The Beast is described as a leopard, bear, and lion (verse 2). These animals represent ancient world empires and are first mentioned in Daniel's prophecy (Daniel 7:4-7). They are mentioned in reverse order there because Daniel was looking ahead to their coming while John was looking back.

The leopard represented the Grecian Empire. The bear symbolized the Medo-Persian Empire, the lion stood for Babylon. The Roman Empire was a combination of all the others. This final kingdom will feature everything that man has been able to construct. It will have the speed of a leopard, the brute strength of a bear, and the majesty of a lion.

This Satanic Superman will receive his power and authority from the devil himself (verse 2).

It is difficult to be dogmatic about verse three. He will apparently suffer a head wound and may stage a seeming resurrection. This will no doubt convince the multitudes of his supernatural power. Since Jesus is the only one resurrected thus far, many will assume that the Beast is actually God. Jesus said he would be so clever as to deceive all but the very elect (Matthew 24:24).

Another possible interpretation of this verse is that it may refer to the Roman Empire. It has been dead or dormant for 1500 years. The Bible speaks alternately of the Beast and his empire and we can easily become confused.

The devil has always wanted to be worshipped. This is what caused him to rebel against God (Isaiah 14:13,14). He will finally get his wish for a brief time (verse 4).

The Beast will have superb speaking abilities (verse 5). Daniel tells us that *"he shall speak great words against the Most High"* (Daniel 7:25). He will be a very charming individual. He will not be a terrorist. He will initially appear to be a man of peace (Daniel 8:25). All of this will be a part of his Satanic deception.

The Antichrist will be in control of world events for 42 months or 3 1/2 years. This will no doubt be the last half of the Tribulation.

He will oppose God and His people (verses 6-7). No mere human will be able to stand against him. He will *"wear out the saints of the Most High"* (Daniel 7:25). The *"saints"* here are those who have responded to the preaching of the 144,000 (Revelation 7:9). The *"Prince of Princes"* or the Lord Jesus is the only One who can overcome him (Daniel 8:25). Jesus will be more than a match for him (Revelation 19:20).

The only ones who will worship and follow the Beast are those whose names are not written in the Lamb's Book of Life (verse 8). The only way to be safe is to accept Jesus Christ as your Lord and Savior.

II. The Second Beast

Most people ignore the fact that there will be two beasts in the Tribulation. We often tend to merge their activities as though there was just one.

The second beast will be a counterfeit Holy Spirit. This is because the Holy Spirit came to testify of Jesus (John 15:26). The second beast will strive to cause earth dwellers to worship the Antichrist (verse 12).

This individual is also known as the *"False Prophet"* (Revelation 19:20). This term indicates that he may very well be connected to the one-world church that will arise.

Thus we see that there is a *"satanic trinity"* composed of the devil and the two beasts. The devil knows nothing better than to imitate God.

This beast will arise from the earth (verse 11). "Earth" would suggest the area around Palestine. Therefore, the second beast could very well be Jewish. He will be a clever religious leader.

He had two horns, but spoke like a dragon (verse 11). He will obviously be a *"wolf in sheep's clothing."* There has been a great deal of false religion being taught in recent years. The False Prophet will be the final development of apostate religion.

"He doeth great wonders...fire came down from heaven" (verse 13). Most people think that if a miracle is performed something must be genuine. Please be aware that the devil can do miracles. Satan called down fire from heaven and burned up Job's sheep and servants (Job 1:16). Pharaoh's magicians were able to duplicate some of the miracles that were performed by Moses (Exodus 7 and 8). The Antichrist will deceive men with *"signs and lying wonders"* (II Thessalonians 2:9).

We cannot go by miracles or supernatural acts as a test that something is of God. We have something far more reliable--the Word of God. If any so-called miracle doesn't line up with the Bible, we can know that it isn't genuine.

The ultimate deception will be "an image of the beast" that will come alive and speak. Those who refuse to worship the image will be killed (verses 14 and 15). King Nebuchadnezzar also had an image constructed and demanded that all worship it or be killed (Daniel 3).

We are not told specifically how the False Prophet gave life to the image so that it could speak. The Greek word for "image" is "eikon" or "icon" as we would spell it today. This word means that the "image" will be an "exact likeness" of the Beast. It could very well be a clone. Scientists have been working diligently to try to clone a human. When it happens, it could very well turn out to be the exact likeness of the Coming Man of Sin.

The "Mark of the Beast" is described in the final verses of the chapter (verses 16-18). This "mark" will be some type of visible engraving. I do not believe it will be a computer chip implanted under the skin. The devil wants no secret followers. This mark will identify you as a loyal supporter of the Antichrist's government.

Once again, we see the deception used by the enemy of mankind. God sealed His evangelists in Revelation 7:4. We must remember that the devil never has an original thought. He attempts to copy God's methods in order to keep men confused. Satan is the ultimate demonic plagiarist.

The "mark" will be given on the forehead or in the right hand. Without this international symbol, you will be unable to buy or sell. This means the world will have a global economy. If the "mark" was only in certain countries, you could simply move to another nation to get away from it.

The world is rapidly moving toward a global financial system. The American dollar will soon become worthless and will be replaced by an international currency.

The Beast will be identified in some way with a number--666 (verse 18). Six is man's number because man was created on the sixth day (Genesis 1:26-1:31). The Beast will be connected to a trinity of sixes. This is the best that fallen man can achieve. If he were truly God, his number would be "777" because seven is the number of completeness.

Many Bible scholars have attempted to explain the significance of 666, but I believe it will not be fully understood until the Tribulation itself.

Those who receive the "mark" will be lost forever (Revelation 14:9-11). It will be the equivalent of the unpardonable sin in the Tribulation.

Conclusion: Evolutionists say that man came from a beast, but we see in this chapter that man is headed toward the Beast. He will be far more powerful than any mere human. No one but Jesus can stop him (Daniel 8:25).

The battle between Christ and the Antichrist will be fought to the finish. If we know the Lord Jesus Christ as our Savior, we will be on the winning side. All other roads will come to a dead end! Neutrality is not an option. Jesus Himself exclaimed, "He that is not with me is against me." (Matthew 12:30).

"Previews of Coming Events" (Revelation 14:1-20)

Introduction - When I was a child, I enjoyed going to the movies. One of the most anticipated times was when previews of coming attractions were shown.

This chapter presents a glimpse of things that will be dealt with more thoroughly in later chapters.

I. The Song of the Righteous (Revelation 14:1-14:5)

The Lamb and the 144,000 witnesses are seen together in this exciting passage. We met these evangelists earlier in chapter seven.

"And they sung as it were a new song" (verse 3). They will not be able to sing the old songs because they refer to things that have already happened. For example, they can't sing, *"When We All Get to Heaven"* because they will already be there.

The only time in the Bible that a man is referred to as a "virgin" is in verse four. These 144,000 servants will be so completely devoted to God that they won't have time to get married and carry on family activities.

"These are they which follow the Lamb whithersoever He goeth" (verse 4). This is what all of us need to be doing. Our mission is to follow Jesus, not to take Him anywhere. Our goal should always be to be in the center of God's will.

II. Angels and Their Message 14:6-14:13)

Perilous times have arrived (II Timothy 3:1) Three angels record messages of warning and coming judgment.

The first angel flies in the midst of heaven, having the message of the everlasting gospel. This preaching will be directed toward every nation, and kindred, and tongue, and people (verse 6). This is a unique situation. Normally, preaching is left to men. In these desperate times, God decides to use an angel.

I have heard preachers say that Jesus can't come and rapture the church until the gospel has been preached to the whole world However, this worldwide witness will take place during the Tribulation. Sending money to a TV preacher will not cause the Lord to come any sooner.

If the gospel message is made available to every man, there will be no excuses for taking the Mark of the Beast. No one can plead ignorance.

The second angel proclaims that *"Babylon is fallen"* (verse 8). The actual downfall of Babylon will not take place until Revelation 17 and 18. The event is pre-viewed or "anticipated" here. God speaks of future events as though they have already happened. Everything is in the present tense to Him.

The third angel warns against taking the Mark of the Beast (verses 9-12). Anyone who takes this mark cannot be saved (verses 10-11).

This passage of scripture teaches eternal punishment of the unrighteous. All who wear the Mark of the Beast will suffer forever with no rest or relief.

There is a major contrast between those who follow the Lamb and those who follow the Beast. It will be far better to reign with Jesus for 1000 years than with the Beast for 3 1/2 years.

"Blessed are the dead which die in the Lord...rest from their labors" (verse 13). This verse has often been used in funeral services. It is a great word of comfort. However, the specific application is to the Tribulation saints. Many of them will be put to death for opposing the Antichrist.

To *"rest from labor"* doesn't mean that Heaven will be a place of idleness. We will have jobs to do (Revelation 22:3). There will be plenty of activity, but no hardships and trouble.

The dead in the Lord are blessed. Blessed people are happy. The righteous dead are in a place of perfect peace. What a comforting hope is given here! The dead in Christ are with the Lord now and will remain with Him until the Rapture. When the Rapture occurs, their bodies will be raised and rejoined with their spirit.

If you have loved ones who have died in Jesus, don't fret about where they are. They are resting in the presence of Jesus. Don't be troubled at the thought of dying. The moment your eyes close in death, you will open your eyes in the presence of your Heavenly Father. Where Jesus dwells, there will be light and peace forever.

III. A Foretaste of Armageddon (14:14-20)

Armageddon has become a frequent visitor to our vocabulary in recent years. The final battle of history will be fought at Armageddon. It is described more fully in Revelation 16 and Revelation 19. The current scripture is a preview of this gigantic conflict.

John sees the Lord Jesus on a white cloud, coming with a sickle to reap the harvest of the earth (verse 14). It is a preview of coming judgment. God knows just when to judge and people will reap just what they have sown.

Harvest time has finally arrived for planet earth (verse 15). The angel announces that the harvest is "ripe." The Greek word for "ripe" means "overripe" or "rotten".

The picture in verses 17 and 18 is that of an individual cutting clusters of grapes off a vine. The ungodly world system is the *"vine of the earth"* (verse 18). The Lord Jesus Christ is the True Vine (John 15). God wants us to bear fruit for His glory.

The chapter closes with an awesome reminder of the fierceness of God's judgment. Blood will flow to the horses' bridles for 1600 furlongs or 200 miles (verse 20). This gives witness to the awful carnage of Armageddon. No wonder that Jesus said that if He did not return and stop it, no flesh would be left (Matthew 24:22).

Conclusion: This chapter reminds us that the world is racing toward a fearful climax. Jesus is still in control and will return at the appropriate moment. Our job is to keep our spiritual bags packed and be ready for His coming.

"Preparation for Judgment" (Revelation 15:1-8)

Introduction - This is the shortest chapter in the book of Revelation. It is an important chapter because we will be introduced to the seven angels who will pour out the final judgments on a Christ-rejecting world.

I. The Jubilation (verses 1-4)

We are again introduced to those who have refused to take the Mark of the Beast or to worship his image (verse 2). They are identified as those who *"had gotten the victory over the beast."* How could these saints be triumphant when they had been killed? At first glance, it appears that the Antichrist had been victorious. In reality, he is only sending them out into eternity to be forever with their Lord. God's viewpoint is different from man's. His ways are higher than our ways (Isaiah 55:9). All of those saints will no doubt receive a martyr's crown (Revelation 2:10).

We notice that they are standing. This position represents victory. They have shed their blood as a testimony of their allegiance to Christ. Perhaps they will sing *"Victory in Jesus"* out of their Heavenly Hymnal.

"And they sing the song of Moses...the song of the Lamb" (verse 3). The *"song of Moses"* represents the first song in the Bible (Exodus 15). It was sung on the eastern bank of the Red Sea. It came after the Lord had drowned Pharaoh's army.

The "song of Moses" indicates physical deliverance. The Tribulation saints have been delivered from their adversary, the Antichrist.

The *"song of the Lamb"* denotes spiritual redemption by the blood of the Lamb. It recalls the great salvation purchased by God's Lamb at Calvary.

The fact that they sing about the Lamb is proof that Jesus Christ is the Eternal God. No man or created being has been praised such as we see here. In our time, great numbers of people are being deceived about the deity of Jesus. He is co-eternal with God. Since Jesus is the only way to Heaven (Acts 4:12), the devil would love to mislead people in order that they would never be saved. Most individuals will talk about an Eternal Being, but they become defensive when you mention the name of Jesus.

We are given three reasons in verse 4 as to why we should fear the Lord and exalt His name:

(1) *"For thou art holy"* - God alone is worthy of worship. Man is a sinner, but God is absolutely holy.

(2) *"All nations...worship before thee"* - All nations have never worshipped God up until this time. There is a day coming when they will bow at His feet (Isaiah 2:2-4).

(3) *"Thy judgment...manifest"* - God is declared here to be righteous in His judgments. He is on the verge of pouring out the final plagues, but He will do so in righteousness. This means He has a right to judge rebellious men.

II. The Judgment (verses 5-8)

"The temple ... in heaven ... was opened ... seven angels came out ... having the seven plagues" (verses 5 and 6).

This is the third time we have been introduced to seven angels at once. There were seven angels to the churches in chapters two and three. Then seven angels were given trumpets to blow (Revelation 8:2). Now we meet the seven angels who will distribute the most awesome judgments yet.

They go forth from the temple in Heaven. In other words, they come from the very presence of Almighty God. We must never forget that God's judgment is a by-product of His holiness.

The wicked on the earth have insulted God. His holiness demands retribution. There is no other remedy.

"And the temple was filled with smoke from the glory of God ... no man was able to enter ... till the seven plagues ... fulfilled" (verse 8). We are on holy ground here. We may never understand this verse completely.

There occurs here a heavenly blackout. Smoke filled the inner temple where God dwells. Smoke is often a symbol of the presence of the Lord in His holiness. Behind the smoke no doubt the heart of God is broken even as the Lord Jesus wept over Jerusalem when He knew they would reject His offer of pardon and love.

Conclusion: When a lost sinner dies and goes to a place of torment, no one grieves as much as our loving Maker. He sent His only begotten Son to keep us from such a fate. However, if people determine to resist God, He will have no other choice.

All of us will go meet our father when we die. If God is our Father, we will enjoy eternity in His presence. The lost will likewise go to live in the presence of their "daddy". The devil is the spiritual father of the unrighteous (John 8:44).

"The Seven Vials of Wrath" (Revelation 16:1-21)

Introduction - The shadows of Armageddon are already upon this troubled planet. Modern weapons of destruction make it possible for man to annihilate himself. Current events seem to be foreshadowing the judgments described in this chapter.

There is a good deal of similarity between these vial judgments and the trumpet judgments earlier in Chapters Eight and Nine. The major difference is that the vial judgments are more severe. These judgments are directed against the Beast and his followers. They will pave the way for the return of Christ to earth to set up His kingdom.

I. The First Vial (verses 1 and 2)

"There fell a noisome and grievous sore upon the men which had the mark of the beast" (verse 2).

Seven angels will be used of God to pour out "vials" or "bowls" of judgment. These plagues demonstrate a preview of what Hell will be like.

The first vial causes a grievous sore on those who have taken the Mark of the Beast. This is "poetic justice" because a sore is an outward sign of inward corruption. These people were already corrupt in their hearts, now this rottenness spreads to the outside.

The original language of the Bible gives the idea that the sores will give off an odor. Some have speculated that the Mark of the Beast could be some type of engraving. If so, it could become infected and thus give forth a foul smell.

Only those who have taken the Mark of the Beast will be punished. God will supernaturally protect His own as He did the children of Israel during the plagues of Egypt.

II. The Second Vial (verse 3)

"Second angel poured out his vial...sea...became as the blood of a dead man" (verse 3).

The rivers of Egypt turned to blood during the first

plague (Exodus 7:20). One-third of the sea turned to blood under the second trumpet judgment (Revelation 8:8).

During this time, the seas of the world will change and become as the blood of a dead man. This will cause a rotten, stinking condition. All sea life will die and decay. This will no doubt lead to all kinds of diseases and infections. Men will search in vain for fresh water.

III. The Third Vial (verses 4-7)

"Third angel poured out his vial...rivers and fountains of waters...became blood" (verse 4).

One river in Egypt turned to blood as commanded by Moses, but here every river on earth turns to blood. Earth's residents will have nothing but blood to drink.

Have you ever been thirsty? If you have never accepted Jesus as your Savior, you are headed for a place where there is no water and never will be. This is why we must give our heart to Jesus without delay.

Unrepentant men may criticize God for sending these plagues, but the angel announces that God is righteous for doing so (verse 5). The reason is given in the next verse. *"For they have shed the blood of saints and prophets"* (verse 6). They will get exactly what they deserve. People reap what they sow (Galatians 6:7). The Antichrist and his followers shed the blood of the saints. Now they will be forced to drink blood.

IV. The Fourth Vial (verses 8 and 9)

"Fourth angel poured out his vial...upon the sun...men were scorched with great heat" (verses 8-9).

The power of the sun will be increased until the enormous heat roasts the backs of men. The Old Testament closes with a similar prediction. *"For, behold, the day cometh, that shall burn as an oven"* (Malachi 4:1). Men and women will have a mass of giant blisters all over them--dried skin burned with great heat.

We have lived through heat waves at one time or another, but things eventually get better. To make matters worse, no water will be available. Man is now able to taste the torments of Hell as described in the story of the rich man and Lazarus (Luke 16:23,24).

We have pretty well destroyed the ozone layer, which protects us from the harmful rays of the sun. Most people had never bothered with sunscreen until recent years. The great increase in skin cancers may be a foretaste of things to come.

V. The Fifth Vial (verses 10 and 11)

"The fifth angel poured out his vial...darkness...gnawed their tongues for pain" (verse 10).

We have another reminder that these vials follow the pattern of the plagues in Egypt in the Book of Exodus. It's interesting that judgment came upon Pharaoh because he mistreated the Jews. The Antichrist will likewise be a tor-mentor of the chosen people.

This darkness may bring some relief from the awful heat wave of the fourth vial. This judgment will focus on the headquarters of the Beast (probably Rome). The contrast be-tween the fourth and fifth vials is startling. One describes scorching brightness from the sun. The other introduces great darkness.

The darkness that falls upon the Antichrist is a symbol of the spiritual darkness which falls upon his followers. Satan is called an *"angel of light"* (II Corinthians 11:14), but God will prevent him from having any illumination in that day.

The last time the earth was completely blacked out was when Jesus hung on the cross. He was paying the sin debt for you and me. He took the sinners place--outer darkness forever.

The Word of God warns about this vial in several scrip-tures. *"The day of the Lord is darkness, and not light"* (Amos 5:18). *"Darkness shall pursue His ene-mies"* (Nahum 1:8). "A day of darkness, and gloominess, a day of clouds and thick darkness" (Zephaniah 1:16). "The sun shall be darkened, and the moon shall not give her light" (Mark 13:24).

These seven vials or bowls of wrath will apparently overlap and cover only a brief period of time. We see an indication of that in verse eleven. We are studying the fifth vial yet we note that men still have their sores. They were poured out under the first vial.

We see another amazing truth here. Despite their suffering, they do not call on the Lord for mercy. Instead, they curse and blaspheme God for His wrath upon them. When men reject the Lord, it is not because of unanswered questions or unexplained events, but hardness of heart and love for sin. Jesus said men love darkness rather than light (John 3:19). They may try to hide behind hypocrites, but the real problem is a wicked heart.

Their very suffering only causes them to despise God even more. The Lord Jesus has told us that in eternity, lost men will not only weep and wail, but also gnash their teeth (Matthew 13:42; Matthew 22:13). The term "gnashing of teeth" indicates rage and anger against a Holy God.

VI. The Sixth Vial (verses 12-16)

"The sixth angel poured out his vial...river Euphrates...dried up" (verse 12).

The Euphrates River is one of the major bodies of water in the world. It is 1800 miles long and was the eastern border of the land God gave to Abraham. This great river had a connection to the Garden of Eden (Genesis 2:14). It was in this region where the Serpent won the first skirmish over Adam and Eve. In this same area, the last battle will be fought. Satan will finally be defeated.

The Euphrates will be dried up to permit "the kings of the east" to get to Armageddon. The Greek word for "east" here literally means "the sun-rising". Japan is known as the kingdom of the rising sun. An earlier reference (Revelation 9:16) mentions an army of 200 million. The only country that could muster up that many soldiers would be Red China. Therefore, China will obviously lead the "kings of the east".

How will these armies be gathered? The satanic trinity is made up of the dragon (Satan), the beast (Antichrist), and the false prophet (imitation Holy Spirit). Like frogs they come from dark places.

These demonic spirits will have power to work miracles to deceive the nations. The "whole world" will be involved, so we can safely call this a global conflict. No nation will remain neutral.

The word *"battle"* (verse 14) is better translated as "campaign". The final conflict of history will not be a one-day affair. The last half of the Tribulation will be a time of extended conflict. A Russian-Islamic invasion of the Holy Land will apparently instigate events leading to Armageddon (Ezekiel 38 and 39).

The prophet Zechariah tells us that all nations will unite for a final assault upon Jerusalem (Zechariah 14:2). We are already beginning to see all the nations backing off from the support of Israel. This Anti-Semitic trend will intensify as we approach the climax of history.

The name "Armageddon" is used only once in the Bible (verse 16). It is also referred to in scripture as the "valley of Megiddo" and the "valley of Jezreel." It is a great valley that runs across northern Israel.

Megiddo was a prominent battlefield of the Old Testament. Gideon, Samson, and David all won great victories there. King Saul and his son, Jonathan, were both slain in this area. Napoleon saw the valley of Armageddon and supposedly said, "All the armies of the world could get in here". One day, they will! It will become a valley of blood for 200 miles (Revelation 14:20).

The whole world will be in conflict, but the major focus will be on Jerusalem and the tiny state of Israel.

The outcome of the battle is not given unto us until the nineteenth chapter.

VII. The Seventh Vial (verses 17-21)

"The seventh angel poured out his vial...voice...from the

throne, saying, It is done" (verse 17).

When the Lord Jesus died at Calvary, He shouted, *"it is finished"* (John 19:30). The plan of salvation was completed.

In this verse, the judgment of the earth was finished. God is going to redeem His creation and boot the usurper (Satan) out.

The closing verses of this chapter describe unprecedented confusion and calamity. The world's greatest earthquake is registered (verse 18). This will be the "big one" that people have been fearing. Some have suggested that this shaking will be the result of the use of weapons of mass destruction.

Jerusalem will be divided into three parts (verse 19), but every major city on earth will be affected. The Mount of Olives will break in half (Zechariah 14:4).

The whole form of the earth will be changed. Every island and mountain range will vanish. In addition, great hailstones about the weight of a talent, will fall from the sky. The word "talent" is thought to be around 100 pounds.

"Men blasphemed God because of the plague of the hail" (verse 21). The Mosaic Law demanded that blasphemers should be stoned (Leviticus 24:16). Almighty God will uphold His law and stone the blasphemers with giant pieces of hail.

Conclusion: You would think by now that everyone would fall on their face and cry out to God for mercy and forgiveness. Instead of repenting, they cursed God for sending judgment on them.

People often say that when these days come, then they will repent. The Bible contradicts that idea. Repentance can only come by conviction of the Holy Spirit. He will not convict those who have continually rebelled against Him.

Man has now "progressed" to the point where he can blow up the entire earth and destroy civilization. A few years ago, men scoffed at the Book of Revelation with its description of terrible judgments. Modern technology has made all of it possible.

The Lord warns of His coming *"as a thief"* in verse fifteen. Here is the promise that you may escape these dreadful events. Are you watching for the coming of the Lord? If not, you have plenty to worry about.

"The Woman and the Beast"
"Religious Babylon" (Revelation 17:1-17:18)

Introduction - This chapter and the one that follows represents another pause in the Book of Revelation. In time se-
quence, the nineteenth chapter immediately follows chapter
sixteen. The apostle John is taken aside to see this amazing
vision of the false church that will exist in the end times.
This chapter appears to be teaching that some type of one-
world church is coming.

This chapter cannot be properly understood without a
correct interpretation of some complex symbols. The two
main symbols are a harlot and a beast with seven heads and
ten horns. We will look at each of them in a topical way.

It's easy to get confused in this chapter, but an angel
helped John to understand (verse 7). May the Holy Spirit
likewise aid us in a correct interpretation.

I. Harlot (Verses 1-6)

The worst thing about the harlot is that she was drunk--
but it wasn't alcohol that contributed to her condition. It was
blood--the blood of believers (verse 6).

When John gets his first peek at the harlot, she was sitting on a weird creature that resembled a television monster.
The monster was just as disgusting to John as the whore. It
had seven heads and ten horns. Perverted, filthy names were
written all over it and it was scarlet, the color of blood.
Sometimes evil things both attract and repel us. As John saw
the wicked woman, he was both fascinated and repulsed. She
was lavishly decked out with gold and precious stones and
pearls. The cup she held in her hand was made of real gold
on the outside, but inside it was filled with vulgar and filthy
things (verse 4).

All the kings of the earth have committed adultery with
her, and she is so perverted she has intoxicated the majority

of earth's residents (verse 2). She is said to *"sit on many waters"*, which is another way of saying that she has control over multitudes of people she has seduced in one way or another. The false religious system will be worldwide in scope. It will be a one-world or global church embracing all religious faiths. It will have its headquarters in a city built on "seven mountains" or hills. It is obviously Rome.

It is clear that we are not dealing with a human being in these verses because no one woman could commit fornication with all the world's leaders nor could she be "drunk with the blood of the saints".

One good rule for understanding the Bible is when the scripture wording makes common sense, don't look for another meaning. In this case, a literal woman would not make sense, so we must seek another sense.

In the Word of God, the terms "whore", "harlot", and "adultery" are often used to represent a spiritual departure from God by a person or country. The word "harlot" may refer to a false religion. For example, Jeremiah condemned the Israelites for following after the false religions of their neighboring countries. *"But thou hast played the harlot with many lovers"* (Jeremiah 3:1). Friendship with the world system is equated to "spiritual adultery" (James 4:4). To flirt with false religion is seen as spiritual adultery because the genuine believer is already engaged to the Lord Jesus Christ (II Corinthians 11:2).

Therefore, we conclude that the harlot woman of this chapter stands for a worldwide false religious system.

"I saw a woman sit upon a scarlet coloured beast" (verse 3). This is the same Beast we studied in chapter 13. For a brief time, the religious system will control the political during the Tribulation. This will only be temporary as we see in verse 16. God has never intended for a global church system to rule until Jesus has returned and set up His kingdom.

The global church will have enormous wealth. She will

be *"decked with gold and precious stones and pearls"* (verse 4). When all the religious bodies unite, the financial combining of resources will be great. We are already seeing the beginning stage of this by the various ecumenical councils being held. It may appear to be a good idea for the religions to unite, but not unless Jesus Christ is the Head.

The woman will be known as *"Mystery Babylon"* (verse 5). Babylon was an ancient city located on the banks of the Euphrates River. The city was begun by Nimrod in Genesis 11. Babylon means "confusion". The men in Nimrod's day were going to build a tower to heaven. They wanted to be independent of God. They sought to build a utopia apart from God.

The Lord stopped the city, scattered the people, and confused their tongues. However, the people did not forget the idol worship Nimrod taught them. The spirit of Nimrod and Babylon is still with us. We call it secular humanism today. It's the old idea that man doesn't need God.

"And I saw the woman drunken with the blood of the saints, and with the blood of the martyrs of Jesus" (verse 6). This verse proves we are not dealing with the true church. A genuine church would not be killing the followers of Christ. A study of church history will reveal that millions have been executed in the name of religion.

II. Beast (Verses 8-18)

"The beast that thou sawest was, and is not; and shall ascend out of the bottomless pit, and go into perdition" (verse 8). Note that he was, is not, and yet shall be. Therefore, the Beast must be one who has lived, was dead at John's time, but would be resurrected later. The fact that he will come out of the bottomless pit suggests that he has been raised from the dead. "Perdition" means "damnation" and links the Antichrist to Judas Iscariot (John 17:12; II Thessalonians 2:3). Some Bible students believe that Antichrist will be Judas raised from the dead.

The Beast has seven heads and ten horns (verse 3). *"The*

seven heads are seven mountains on which the woman sitteth" (verse 9). As stated earlier, the headquarters of the one-world church will be a city with seven mountains or hills. This would be Rome.

"And there are seven kings: five are fallen, and one is, and the other is not yet come" (verse 10). Five kingdoms had already fallen--Egypt, Assyria, Babylon, Persia, and Greece. "One is"--that was the present kingdom of Rome. "The other that is not yet come" would be the Revived Roman Empire which would arise in the last days.

"And the beast that was, and is not, even he is the eighth, and is of the seven, and goeth into perdition" (verse 11). The Beast will institute the eighth and final form of the Revived Roman Empire. He will be the "eighth" ruler, but he is from the seventh kingdom.

The ten horns are ten kingdoms that shall arise out of the old Roman Empire. This corresponds with Daniel 2 and 7. They will receive power or authority one hour with the Beast --meaning a certain period of time.

"The ten horns...upon the beast...hate the whore, and shall make her desolate and naked" (verse 16). An interesting shift occurs here. The Antichrist will permit the one-world church to run things for a while. That is why the woman was riding on the back of the Beast earlier (verse 3). After the Antichrist has gained enough clout, he and his ten kings will throw off the harlot because no political leader enjoys taking orders from religious leaders. The Antichrist will no doubt be interested in confiscating the monetary assets of the global church.

How are the mighty fallen. First, the harlot will be hated. She is despised by those who once worshipped her. Second, she will be made desolate, or stripped of her possessions.

Third, she will be made naked. Her shame will be noted by all. Fourth, her enemies will eat her flesh or devour her riches. Fifth, she will be burned with fire, which means social and political ruin.

"For God hath put in their hearts to fulfill his will... give their kingdom unto the beast, until the words of God shall be fulfilled" (verse 17). The Beast and his puppets are simply God's instruments in destroying His enemies. We see another evidence that the kingdoms of this world are simply fitting into God's master plan. Rulers and nations cannot change the course of human history. They only fit into God's plan for the world. God is sovereign in history.

"And the woman which thou sawest...great city" (verse 18). We should not be surprised that the woman and the religious system are both referred to as a city. The Holy City is also described as a bride in Revelation 21.

The *"harlot woman" "reigned over the kings."* Jesus told Pilate that His kingdom was not of this world (John 18:36).

Conclusion: When Jesus returns the Second Time, He will establish His earthly kingdom. Whenever the church as an organization has gotten into politics, she has become spiritually sidetracked. That doesn't rule out individual Christians voting and being good citizens.

"When God Comes to Wall Street"
"The World Economic Meltdown" (Revelation 18)

Introduction - In the previous chapter, we saw the destruction of religious Babylon--the coming one-world church. In this chapter, we see the downfall of commercial Babylon--the coming global economy.

There must be a global economy or one-world economic system in the end times or else the Mark of the Beast would be a joke. Remember that the Mark will be necessary to *"buy or sell"* (Revelation 13:17).

We hear much talk today of a coming "new world order." The question on everyone's mind is "When will the global society be initiated and who will be in control?" The Book of Revelation answers both concerns. The global economy will become a reality during the Tribulation and the Antichrist will emerge as the world leader.

World financial leaders are currently working diligently to bring to pass a global currency. Globalism is now a "politically correct" concept.

This chapter is more relevant than ever.

I. Reasons for Destruction (Verses 1-7)

John sees a powerful angel come down from Heaven (verse 1). This angel is so glorious that he lightens up the whole world. Many think this angel to be the Lord Jesus.

The angel pronounces judgment or destruction upon Babylon because it represents everything that is against God. When he says *"Babylon the great is fallen, is fallen"* (verse 2), it means both the religious system (chapter 17) and the economic system (chapter 18) will be destroyed. The Greek word used here for "fallen" means that it will happen suddenly. The destruction is said to occur in only "one hour" (verses 10, 17).

We know this is an economic system because the merchants will profit from it (verse 3). Many people will do any-thing for money. *"The love of money is the root of all evil"* (I Timothy 6:10).

God calls on His people to come out and separate them-selves from this humanistic system (verse 4). "Love not the world, neither the things that are in the world" (I John 2:15).

This world is not our home, and we will suffer eternal loss if we become obsessed with earthly possessions. The call to separation has come to the people of God down through the ages. It came to Abraham (Genesis 12:1), to Lot (Genesis 19), and to Israel (Jeremiah 50:8). We are not to be unequally yoked with the ungodly. (II Corinthians 6:14).

"For her sins have reached unto heaven, and God hath remembered her iniquities" (verse 5). "Reached" means to be "glued together". This is a play on words. The original residents of Babylon were determined to build a tower to heaven (Genesis 11). They have finally succeeded, but their "tower' is made of sin that has reached the very nostrils of God.

God will remember all iniquity unless it has been con-fessed and put under the blood of Jesus. What He has for-given will never be used against us (Hebrews 8:12).

II. Reality of Destruction (Verses 8-24)

One truth that stands out in this passage is the sudden-ness of God's judgment. *"Therefore shall her plagues come in one day"* (verse 8). "For in one hour is thy judgment come" (verse 10). *"For in one hour so great riches is come to naught"* (verse 17). God's judgment will be sure, swift, and final.

The greatest economic meltdown in the history of the world is described in these verses. The stock market crash of 1929 will pale in comparison.

This scenario should be obvious as we see America and other nations spending money as if there were no tomorrow. Politicians can only be elected as they promise voters more and more. In the meantime, our future is in economic peril.

Destruction will come quickly and just when Babylon thinks she is a queen (verse 7).

The remainder of the chapter deals with the reactions of different groups of people in regard to the global economic disorder.

Earthly leaders will mourn and lament (verses 9 and 10). The collapse of the New World Order will affect political chieftains because their hope of establishing a humanistic utopia will be dashed. Economic summits will be futile at this time. When Almighty God visits Wall Street, rulers will have nowhere to rule.

Business leaders will likewise express grieving when economic systems tumble. *"And the merchants of the earth shall weep and mourn over her; for no man buyeth their merchandise any more"* (verse 11). The source of their wealth has been destroyed.

Jesus cautioned us as to the folly of laying up worldly treasures. *"But lay up for yourselves treasures in Heaven...For where your treasure is, there will your heart be also"* (Matthew 6:20, 21).

A list of 28 articles are mentioned as being affected (verses 12 and 13). These products are found in various areas of the earth, thus proving that it is a global system. All of them could be considered luxuries except the last--the souls of men. What value would it be to gain the whole world but lose your soul? (Mark 8:36)

Religion is today making merchandise of the souls of men. The so-called "prosperity gospel" is spreading like wildfire. People are being told that they will receive great material blessing by sending money to the televangelists. Not a word is said about repentance and holiness. When preachers lie to people, they are making merchandise of the souls of men.

In contrast to the political and economic leaders, God's people will rejoice when Babylon falls (verses 20-24). Christians and non-Christians do not see things in the same way.

There will be joy in Heaven while there is grief on the earth.

The main reason for Heaven's delight is that God has avenged the blood of the martyrs (verse 20). We met these saints under the fifth seal in Revelation 6:9-11. They had questioned the Lord, *"How long, O Lord, holy and true, dost thou not judge and avenge our blood on them that dwell on the earth?" "Vengeance is mine; I will repay, saith the Lord"* (Romans 12:19).

A mighty angel then takes a millstone and casts it into the sea (verse 21). Many Bible students connect this event with the stone that will destroy the end-time world empire in Daniel 2:44,45.

To indicate the finality of the judgment upon the Babylonian system, there are five "no more" statements (verses 21-23). When God says "no more" it indicates a "done deal". Man will be unable to change the decree of the Lord. God made a similar prediction against Judah in Jeremiah's day (Jeremiah 25:9-11). Man's kingdom will be "no more" but God's kingdom will be just beginning.

Conclusion: Every material thing that men have worked for will be destroyed when the global economy is demolished. There will be "no more" earthly pleasures. Heaven will also be a place of "no mores". There will be no more tears, no more death, no more sorrow, no more crying, and no more pain (Revelation 21:4).

We have seen the destruction of the coming one-world church and the future one-world economy. All that remains is the judgment against the world's armies. That will be described in the next chapter.

"The Chorus and the Coming" (Revelation 19:1-21)

Introduction - This is a chapter of rejoicing. It reveals the ultimate triumph of good over evil, Christ over Antichrist, and God over Satan. The chapter deals with two suppers--the Marriage Supper of the Lamb and the supper of the great God. We will find in these verses the long-anticipated return of the Lord Jesus.

The Hallelujah Chorus from Handel's *Messiah* is one of the most beautiful expressions of praise in the history of music. This passage was the source of Handel's inspiration.

I. The Chorus (Verses 1-10)

We find here the ultimate Hallelujah Chorus in Heaven. The word "Alleluia" or "Hallelujah" means "Praise the Lord." It is one of the few words that is the same in every language. The word is used here four times (verses 1,3,4,6). It is not found anywhere else in the New Testament.

"For He hath judged the great whore...hath avenged the blood of His servants" (verse 2). Do the people in Heaven know what is happening on earth? They do in this case. The enemy is judged and we are free from the great harlot forever.

"And her smoke rose up for ever and ever" (verse 3). This verse affirms the reality of eternal torment. As long as God lives, so long must His wrath be poured out on the wicked.

We meet the 24 elders again (verse 4). We studied them in chapter four. Their cry will be *"Amen; Alleluia."* "Amen" means "let it be so". Jesus used it often with the identical word translated as "verily".

From the tone of these verses, we can safely conclude that Heaven will be a noisy place. It will be no time to be dignified when multitudes of redeemed people of all nations will be giving Him praise. The sound will be like *"mighty thunderings"* (verse 6). Both Heaven and Hell will have a lot of noise. This world is probably the quietest it's going to be.

The Marriage Supper of the Lamb is described in verses seven through nine. This great event is overlooked in most preaching today. It will apparently be one of the two great events that will take place in Heaven while the Tribulation is unfolding on earth. The Marriage Supper will likely be preceded by the Judgment Seat of Christ (Romans 14:10-12).

The Marriage of the Lamb means that Jesus is getting married. I was in church for years and did not know that! The Lamb is Jesus (John 1:29).

Who will Jesus marry? The bride is the church, made up of all the redeemed. Every born-again person will make up the bride. *"For I am jealous over you with godly jealousy: for I have espoused you to one Husband, that I may present you as a chaste virgin to Christ"* (II Corinthians 11:2). Christ and the church are pictured as bride and groom in Ephesians 5:23-32.

The true church is currently engaged to the Lord Jesus. That is why we are guilty of *"spiritual adultery"* if we love the same world system that crucified our fiancé. *"Ye adulterers and adulteresses, know ye not that the friendship of the world is enmity with God?"* (James 4:4)

The church is both the body and bride of Christ. Eve was of the body of Adam and also his bride. Jesus loved the church and gave Himself for it (Ephesians 5:25). She is the *"pearl of great price"* for which He sold all that He had (Matthew 13:46).

The bride's wedding gown is referred to in verse 8. *"And to her was granted that she should be arrayed (dressed) in fine linen, clean and white: for the fine linen is the righteousness of saints."* The word for "righteousness" here is in the plural. It refers to the righteous or godly deeds that we do for the Lord. In other words, we will make our own garment to wear to the Marriage Supper. A person who does little for the Lord after being saved will show up in a heavenly mini-skirt. Salvation is by grace, but our wedding dress will be composed of our good works. It will be embarrassing to show up in a "mini-skirt" before the Lord of the universe.

The groom will be Jesus and the bride will be the Church, but there will also be guests at the wedding. *"Blessed are they which are called unto the marriage supper of the Lamb"* (verse 9). The "called" does not refer to the bride because she doesn't have to be invited to her own wedding. This obviously refers to the wedding guests. John the Baptist indicated that he was a *"friend of the bridegroom"* (John 3:29). The guests would therefore seem to be the Old Testament saints. The Old Testament believers were concerned with earthly rewards, but it is the New Testament Church that will be the bride.

After the marriage comes the honeymoon. Our "honeymoon" will be 1000 years of reigning during the Millennium. Afterwards, He will take us to our permanent home, the New Jerusalem (Revelation 21:2). We will live happily ever after.

John became so excited that he fell at the feet of the angel who showed him these things (verse 10). He repeats this mistake in the final chapter (Revelation 22:8). The angel quickly corrects the old apostle--*"See thou do it not."* The Bible is very clear that we are to worship God only. The fact that Jesus accepted the worship of others means that He and the Father are co-equal (John 20:28). We must never bow before another human being in worship for that would be idolatry.

II. The Coming (Verses 11-21)

"And I saw heaven opened" (verse 11). In Revelation 4:1, a door was opened in heaven. This first opening was in order that we could go up (Rapture). Now heaven is opened so we can return with the Lord Jesus to Armageddon. This second coming is known as the Revelation of Jesus Christ.

This heavenly rider will be seated on a white horse. We

may contrast this rider with the false Christ in Revelation 6:2. The rider in Revelation 19:11 comes from heaven. No earth-born individual can qualify as the Messiah. This eliminates a host of religious pretenders throughout history.

There is quite a contrast between the first and second comings of Christ. He had a lowly birth the first time. He will return in power and glory. He came the first time to a tree. He will come the second time to a throne.

Jesus is identified here as *"Faithful and True."* He was called *"the faithful and true witness"* in the letter to the church at Laodicea (Revelation 3:14).

He will judge and make war in righteousness. He is a powerful conqueror and also a righteous judge. Paul told the intellectuals in Athens that *"He will judge the world in righteousness"* (Acts 17:31). The Judge of all the earth will do what is right (Genesis 18:25). No one will be powerful enough to bribe Him and He will have all the facts.

"His eyes were as a flame of fire, and on his head were many crowns" (verse 12). Revelation 1:14 also states that *"His eyes were as a flame of fire."* No one will be able to hide from him.

The Greek word for "crowns" here is "diadema." This term means He will have all authority because He is the rightful king.

The final phrase in verse 11 is rather difficult to interpret. *"He had a name written, that no man knew, but He Himself."* Perhaps the Gospel of Matthew can help us. *"No man knoweth the Son, but the Father; neither knoweth any man the Father, save the Son"* (Matthew 11:27). The passage is teaching us that our limited minds cannot fully understand an eternal God. We can use words like Lord and Savior to express the relationship between God and His Children. However, Christ the Son in the fullness of His divine nature and eternal existence can only be known by the Father. In other words, we will never be as smart as God.

"He was clothed with a vesture dipped in blood: and his

name is called The Word of God" (verse 13). Blood is such a prominent component of our salvation. *"Without shedding of blood is no remission"* (Hebrews 9:22). A prominent preacher once said that if we cut the Bible at any place, it will bleed.

He is further identified as *"The Word of God."* "In the beginning was the Word, and the Word was with God, and the Word was God" (John 1:1). That same Word became flesh (John 1:14). Jesus is called "The Word of God" because a word is an expression of an idea. Jesus is the image, or exact likeness, of the invisible God (Colossians 1:15).

Heavenly armies riding upon white horses will accompany the Lord Jesus on that glorious day (verse 14). The word "armies" is in the plural. Perhaps it is suggestive of angels and the raptured church. Their clothing was fine linen, white and clean.

These "armies" will actually not have to fight. All of that will be left to our glorious leader, the Lord Jesus Christ. We will watch and cheer Him on.

His only weapon will be a sharp sword that proceeds out of His mouth (verse 15). The Word of God is sharper than a two-edged sword (Hebrews 4:12). *"He shall smite the earth with the rod of His mouth, and with the breath of His lips shall He slay the wicked"* (Isaiah 11:4). He will speak with such authority that victory is assured.

Do you now understand the importance of the Word of God? It will be the weapon that will bring the ultimate downfall of the devil. That's why Satan's initial attack on mankind was to challenge God's Word (Genesis 3:1).

When tempted by the devil, Jesus relied on the Word of God--*"It is written"* (Matthew 4:4-10). The Word of God is my assurance of salvation.

Jesus will rule the nations *"with a rod of iron."* "Thou shalt break them with a rod of iron" (Psalms 2:9). Jesus will not be up for re-election every four years. He will be neither a Democrat or Republican. He will rule with total authority.

He will reveal Himself as *"KING OF KINGS, AND LORD OF LORDS"* (verse 16). The Name says it all! He will possess all the kingdoms of the world and He will govern with perfect justice. At last, Isaiah's prophecy will be completed. *"The government shall be upon His shoulder"* (Isaiah 9:6).

Queen Victoria ruled Great Britain longer than any other monarch (1837-1901). One day a chaplain spoke at the palace about this verse. The Queen was so moved that she exclaimed, *"O That He would come today. I would love to lay my crown at His feet." "At the name of Jesus every knee should bow...And that every tongue should confess that Jesus Christ is Lord"* (Philippians 2:10-11).

The closing verses of this great chapter deal with another supper--the supper of the great God (verse 17). Birds will be invited to devour the flesh of those who dared to fight against God Himself (verse 18). This "supper" will climax the campaign of Armageddon. The Lord Jesus graphically warned of this feast when He proclaimed, *"For wheresoever the carcase is, there will be eagles (vultures) be gathered together"* (Matthew 24:28). The armies of mankind will unite in a futile attempt to prevent the Lord and His army from returning to earth (verse 19). They think they will destroy tiny Israel (Zechariah 14:2), but they will fall into God's plan to destroy the wicked in the Valley of Jehoshaphat (Joel 3:2). This area is on the east side of Jerusalem and is known as the Kidron Valley at the present time.

The creature is foolish indeed to war against His Creator. In recent years we have seen evidence of man's rebellion against the Almighty. God has been systematically eliminated from the public schools. Christ has been removed from Christmas. Man's hostility toward God will grow more fervent as the clock of history winds down.

The Beast and the False Prophet (Second Beast of Revelation 13) were both cast alive into a *"lake of fire"* (verse 20). Two men in the Old Testament, Enoch and Elijah, were taken to Heaven without physical death. Likewise, the two Beasts will go to Hell without physically dying.

Conclusion: It is an imperative that all of us must choose to be at one of these two suppers. If you have been saved, you will be seated at the Marriage Supper of the Lamb where all is gladness and singing. But if you neglect His grace, you will not have a meal, but instead you will become a meal.

Those at the Marriage Supper will have an endless hope. The others have a hopeless end.

"The Millennial Kingdom" (Revelation 20:1-15)

Introduction - There are two major events discussed in this vital chapter--the Millennial Kingdom and the Great White Throne Judgment.

This is often referred to as the "thousand year" chapter. We know it as the Millennium. "Millennium" means "thousand years" in Latin. The expression "thousand years" occurs six times--in every verse from verse two through verse seven.

A phrase from the Model or Lord's Prayer tells us to pray for *"Thy kingdom come"* (Matthew 6:10). This is the Kingdom to which Christ was referring. During this thousand year reign, God will fulfill the Old Testament promises made to the nation of Israel. There is a false teaching today that maintains that the church has replaced Israel; therefore, we may claim the promises God made to the Jews. This is an example of wrongly dividing scripture. If God did not keep His promises to the Jews, how could we depend on Him to keep His promises to the Gentiles?

The prophet Isaiah has much to say about this blessed time. Texts that would interest the student of prophecy would be Isaiah 2:2-4; 11:6-9; and chapter 65. Nations will beat their swords into plowshares and their spears into pruning hooks (Isaiah 2:4). There will be no war. This will enable countries to divert their military budgets and use the same money to support agriculture to feed the hungry. The animal kingdom will be at peace. The wolf and lamb will lie down in harmony (Isaiah 11:6). Long life will be restored as it was in the early days of Genesis. A 100 year old man will still be considered a child (Isaiah 65:20).

Jesus will rule from Jerusalem (Isaiah 2:3) and Israel will become the leading nation in the world.

I. The Millennial Kingdom (Verses 1-10)

A mighty angel comes down from heaven with a key to the *"bottomless pit"* and a great chain in his other hand. He grabs hold of the devil and locks him up in the "bottomless pit" for 1000 years. This is the major reason there will be peace on earth--the devil won't be around to bother anyone. We could perhaps have peace today if the devil became imprisoned.

There is much speculation that the angel is Jesus. This is so crucial that I wonder if God would entrust it to anyone else or even if anyone else was able. Satan seems to have more authority than anyone except Jesus.

How can you bind a spirit being? It was obviously not a physical chain or else the old Dragon might escape. This chain will be adequate to hold the ruler of spiritual darkness.

We see four names or titles for our defendant in verse 2. He is called dragon, serpent, devil, Satan. He is a "con artist" who operates under many titles.

The devil's penitentiary is identified as the *"bottomless pit"* (verse 3). It's also known as the Abyss or "the deep." It is not the final Lake of Fire.

A seal was placed on the devil so that he might not escape for 1000 years. When the Lord Jesus was lain in the tomb, they set a seal upon Him in a futile attempt to keep Him in the grave.

"And I saw thrones...judgment was given unto them...souls of them that were beheaded for the witness of Jesus...lived and reigned with Christ a thousand years" (verse 4). We met these tribulation martyrs under the fifth seal (Revelation 6:9-11). God has finally got around to punishing those who were responsible for their deaths. When the Lord pays, He pays in full.

The first resurrection is highlighted in verses 5 and 6. The Bible does not teach a general resurrection where saved and lost will appear together. Those in the first resurrection are said to be *"Blessed and holy."* They will reign with Christ for a thousand years. The lost will be judged at the second resurrection which will be at least a thousand years later (verse 5).

The first resurrection will be in three installments:

(1) Christ is the firstfruits (I Corinthians 15:20). Because He lives we can be assured the grave will not hold us.

(2) The church will be raised at the Rapture (I Thessalonians 4:16,17). This will occur in the twinkling of an eye (I Corinthians 15:52).

(3) Tribulation saints and Old Testament saints will be brought forth at the end of the Tribulation (Revelation 20:4).

"When the thousand years are expired, Satan shall be loosed" (verse 7). The devil will be let out of his prison at the close of the Millennial Kingdom. This has been a puzzle to many. After all, we were getting along fine without him.

The obvious question is "Why would God release the devil?" We must recall that when Jesus returned and destroyed the wicked during the war of Armageddon, everyone was not killed. Some had not taken the Mark of the Beast and they were spared. They entered the Millennial Kingdom in a natural body. We will enter in a spiritual body.

The Tribulation survivors will be able to marry and have children. There will be a population explosion because there will be no war to kill them off. Satan's release will permit him to tempt those born during the thousand years. These people have never had to choose between good and evil. All they have ever known is Jesus and His government. They went along with Jesus because He was stronger.

"And shall go out to deceive the nations...the number of whom is as the sand of the sea" (verse 8).

We note first of all that a thousand years in prison has not changed the devil one bit. He continues to hate God and His people.

You might think that after a thousand years of peace and prosperity that no one would follow the devil anyway. However, the Word of God says his followers will be as numerous as *"the sand of the sea."* If this takes you by surprise, just remember Adam and Eve. They listened to the devil even though they lived in a perfect environment. They rebelled against God even though they lived in a state of paradise.

Please understand that we will not be tempted by the devil after we get to Heaven. This temptation will only be for those born during the thousand years of the Millennial Kingdom.

Almighty God will destroy this rebellion by sending down fire from heaven (verse 9). A famous preacher once said, "Your arms are too short to box with God".

What will happen to the leader of this revolt? The devil will be cast into a lake of fire and brimstone (verse 10). Finally, the old deceiver will arrive at his final destination. This is the reason Hell was created--for the devil and his angels (Matthew 25:41). The devil will not be the "boss" of Hell. Rather, he will be its chief victim. God has the ultimate authority over hell. Jesus declared that He had the keys of Hell (Revelation 1:18).

We must not overlook another key fact in this verse. The beast and the false prophet were still there when Satan arrived. They had been cast into the fire over a thousand years earlier (Revelation 19:20). Some cults teach that the souls of the wicked would be annihilated or burned up. Yet we find here two men who have been in torment for over a thousand years and they haven't burned up.

Hell will be a place of eternal suffering. Its residents will be *"tormented day and night for ever and ever."* We must come to this understanding--if Hell is not eternal, neither is Heaven. The same Greek word is used to refer to both in Matthew 25:46.

The Book of Revelation is the only resource as to the destiny of the devil. No wonder the evil one hates this prophecy. Satan will be mentioned no more. The late Vance Havner once said, "Thank God for a Bible where the devil is not mentioned in the first two chapters nor the last two chapters."

II. The Great White Throne (Verses 11-15)

This is perhaps the most awesome scripture in all the Bible. It is a description of the final judgment. All lost people will be here to receive the news of their eternal destiny. It is sometimes referred to as the "Court of Last Resort." There will be no defense nor appeal in regard to this verdict.

We saw earlier a throne with a rainbow over it (Revelation 4:3). The rainbow is symbolic of mercy. The unsaved will appear at the Great White Throne. No mercy will be extended at this throne.

Lost folks could have settled their case out of court. My case was settled at Calvary when the Lord Jesus paid for my sins in full. *"There is therefore now no condemnation to them which are in Christ Jesus"* (Romans 8:1). There are only two places where God deals with sin in a judicial way-- Calvary and the Great White Throne. If your sins were not put on Christ, then you must face them yourself.

"And I saw a great white throne...Him that sat on it" (verse 11). The throne is "great" because lost individuals neglect a great salvation (Hebrews 2:3). "White" represents holiness or purity.

The Judge at this final day of Court will be none other than the Lord Jesus Christ. Many scriptures attest to this fact (John 5:22; Acts 17:31; Romans 2:16). This Judge will have all the facts and will render His verdict based on justice.

"From whose face the earth and the heaven fled away." There will be no place to hide. Many today delight in taking refuge behind the hypocrites. The defendants will be speechless before Judge Jesus (Romans 3:19).

"And I saw the dead, small and great, stand before God...books were opened...dead were judged...according to their works" (verse 12). All kinds of sinners will be there. Every social class will be represented. Good moral people will be there as well as the most vile sinner.

People are deceived into thinking that their morality will gain them a home in Heaven. In order for a person to enter

Heaven by works, they would have to be as holy as Almighty God. Their case is hopeless because the best we can do is as *"filthy rags"* before a righteous God (Isaiah 64:6).

The dead will be judged from God's books. He is keeping an accurate record of every person's life. Those who have trusted Christ will find their sins edited out (Hebrews 10:17), but the lost will face every sin they have committed.

Perhaps rocks or nature shall testify against the unredeemed. Joshua challenged his generation to serve God by setting up a stone before the people. If they broke their pledge, the stone would witness against them (Joshua 24:27). Jesus warned that the rocks would cry out in praise to Him if man kept silent (Luke 19:40). Their sentence will be *"according to their works."* It will determine the degree of punishment. It will be based on the amount of light or understanding a person had.

"Sea gave up the dead which were in it" (verse 13). Many people have drowned at sea during the centuries. God knows where those bodies are. Many have been cremated and their ashes have been scattered over the waters. God the Creator will bring them up for judgment.

"Death and hell delivered up the dead which were in them." The word "death" here means "grave" or "cemetery". The word "hell" means "Hades" or the place where a lost soul goes after death. When an unsaved person dies, their body goes to the grave and their soul goes to a place of torment (Hades). At the Great White Throne, soul and body will be brought back together.

The lost dead will be judged *"according to their works."* The Bible teaches degrees of punishment for the wicked. No doubt this will be dependent on the amount of wickedness, light refused, etc.

"Death and hell were cast into the lake of fire...second death" (verse 14). One scholar calls this "The death of death." Death will finally be eliminated. This is man's most feared enemy (I Corinthians 15:26).

The "second death" is a term used here. Physical death is the separation of the soul from the body (James 2:26). The second death or spiritual death occurs when the soul and body are separated from God. We are born once to die twice or we are born twice to die once. If you have never been born again, you have yet to face two deaths. Most people don't like to talk about the first, much less the second.

"Whosoever was not found...book of life...cast into the lake of fire" (verse 15). The Book of Life will contain the names of all the redeemed. Once your name is recorded there, it can never be erased (Revelation 3:5). The important thing is not which church you belong to, but whether your name is in God's Book. Accepting Jesus as your personal Savior is the only way to be sure your name is written in the Book of Life.

Conclusion: There is no need to be at the Great White Throne. You may settle your case out of court. The Philippian jailer asked, *"What must I do to be saved?"* Paul responded by saying, *"Believe on the lord Jesus Christ, and thou shalt be saved"* (Acts 16:30,31).

Jesus went to a great deal of trouble so that we could avoid this final judgment. The time to call on Him is today (II Corinthians 6:2).

"The Eternal Kingdom" (Revelation 21 and 22)

Introduction - The final two chapters will be examined together as they deal with the same theme and that is "The Eternal Kingdom".

Jesus had told His disciples that He was going away to prepare a place for them (John 14:2,3). In this section, we are granted a glimpse of that place. We are citizens of two worlds, both come by birth.

Everybody looks forward to a "new home." If I were moving to Israel to live the rest of my life, I'd try to learn all I could about that country before I got there. I'd study its history, its geography, its people, its language, its customs, and its government. I'd be interested in life in Israel.

Because I intend to live in Heaven forever, I have an interest in that country. I want to learn as much as I can about it now.

I. The New Heaven and the New Earth (21:1-7)

"And I saw a new heaven and a new earth: for the first heaven and the first earth were passed away" (Revelation 21:1). The Lord Jesus had warned that *"Heaven and earth shall pass away, but my word shall not pass away"* (Matthew 24:35). *"For behold, I create new heavens and a new earth"* (Isaiah 65:20).

"And I John saw the holy city...coming down out of heaven" (verse 2). The new heaven and the new earth are not described, but the Illuminated City is. The New Jerusalem will apparently be suspended between the new heaven and the new earth. This will be our new headquarters but we will be able to visit the renovated earth as well.

The city will be prepared "as a bride." The church is the bride of Christ, but the city here is compared to a bride. A city is known by its people. Everything will be beautiful just as a bride on her wedding day.

"For here have we no continuing city" (Hebrews 13:14). Earthly cities rise and fall, but the new Jerusalem will be the eternal residence of the redeemed.

"God Himself shall be with them, and be their God" (verse 3). God now abides in Paradise or the third heaven. He will move His headquarters to the new Jerusalem. In other words, God Himself will be our next door neighbor. How could we ever know fear if the Lord is living next to us? He once came down and walked with Adam daily (Genesis 3:8). Our fellowship will be more intimate than that. Our mansions will truly be built next door to Jesus.

"And God shall wipe away all tears...no more death...nor crying, neither shall there be any more pain" (verse 4). This is one of the most comforting verses in the Bible. It reinforces the concept that Heaven will be worth it all. No one will ever lose by trusting Christ.

God will take out His "heavenly handkerchief" and wipe the final tear from our eye. Death will be unknown in that celestial city. No funeral homes will be needed there. Man's final enemy, death, will be abolished (I Corinthians 15:26).

It's amazing how the devil deceives people into thinking they have to give up too much to be saved. What we "lose" is death, sorrow, crying, and pain. A little girl once saw a cross on the communion table. She asked her mother, "What's that plus sign doing there?" Christians come out ahead, both here and in eternity.

"Behold, I make all things new" (verse 5). We all enjoy new things. Nothing in Heaven will be recycled. It will all be original.

Those who are spiritually thirsty may drink of the water of life freely (verse 6). This invitation will be given again later (Revelation 22:17).

The overcomer will *"inherit all things"* (verse 7). *"I will be his God, and he shall be my son."* We will never become gods ourselves. I am satisfied to be one of His children. The devil tricked Eve into thinking that she could be equal with God (Genesis3:5). There is and always will be only one God, but we can become His children if we receive Christ Jesus as our Savior (John 1:12,13).

II. A Hopeless Neighborhood (Revelation 21:8)

This is a negative verse in the midst of eternal surroundings. If you are moving into a new area, you want to be acquainted with the neighbors. This verse is referred to as "Hell's Neighborhood". It is a hopeless community because no one will ever move out. Thus, there is no possibility for improvement. Eight groups are identified as being residents of this hopeless subdivision.

A. Fearful - Isn't it interesting that the "fearful" are listed first. It refers to those who are afraid to accept Jesus. Their pride will trip them up.

B. Unbelieving - Those who have never been "born again" (John 3:5).

C. Abominable - These are the filthy and perverted people who seem to always be in the news.

D. Murderers - All those who are guilty of shedding innocent blood throughout history.

E. Whoremongers - Those guilty of sexual abuse or idolatry.

F. Sorcerers - This would include various types of witchcraft and black magic. The Greek word here would also refer to those involved in drugs.

G. Idolaters - An idol is anything you love more than you love God. *"Thou shalt have no other gods before me"* (Exodus 20:3).

H. Liars - All who practice lying as a lifestyle will end up in the lake of fire.

There will be three more residents who were described earlier--the devil, beast, and false prophet. This is why Hell was created anyway (Matthew 25:41). All others will go there as intruders.

III. The Pearly White City (Revelation 21:9-27)

Many Gospel songs have been written about Heaven. Much of their material has been taken from this passage. No one will be able to appreciate its beauty until they get there (Isaiah 64:4). We will summarize its major features.

John is carried away in the spirit and is given a vision of our heavenly home (verse 10). Some may argue that the city is the bride of Christ, but a city is known by its people. Born -again believers will make up the bride.

The new Jerusalem will be a *"gated city"* (verse 12). There will be twelve gates with angels stationed there as our *"greeters"* (verses 12-13). There is only one way to Heaven, but there is an abundant entrance into the city.

We will always be reminded of our debt to the Jew. The names of the twelve tribes of Israel will be inscribed on the gates. We owe much to the Hebrew people. They have given us the Son of God and the Word of God. *"Salvation is of the Jews"* (John 4:22).

"And the twelve gates were twelve pearls: every several gate was of one pearl" (verse 21). The "pearly gates" will remind us of suffering. An oyster goes through a great deal of pain to produce a pearl. The oyster must be wounded before the pearl can be formed. The Lord Jesus was *"wounded for our transgressions"* (Isaiah 53:5). Our salvation was purchased at a great price.

The only man-made thing in Heaven will be the marks in the body of the Lord Jesus. We will never forget what He did for us at Calvary.

The gates of Heaven will never be shut (verse 25). The redeemed will be free to come and go as they please. No curfew will need be imposed because there will be no night there. The wall of the city will be 144 cubits high or 216 feet as a cubit equals 18 inches (verse 17). Because of its enormous height, the wall will need twelve foundations (verse 14). The foundations will remind us of the New Testament saints. The names of the twelve apostles will be listed on the foundations. It will be interesting to see who the twelfth apostle will be. Many Bible scholars think it will be Paul. We'll have to wait and see.

The foundations will each be decorated with stones (verses 19-20). The stones will vary in color and give a rainbow-type appearance. The high priest in the Old Testament had a breastplate with twelve stones that represented the twelve tribes of Israel.

The dimensions of the Pearly White City are magnificent. The city will be four square (verse 16). It will be twelve thousand furlongs in length, width, and height. A furlong is a little over 600 feet. When the calculations are determined, the city will be approximately 1500 miles in every direction. Modern airplanes fly about 7-8 miles high. This city will tower into the air for 1500 miles. No earthly city can compare to the new Jerusalem of God. There will be plenty of room for the redeemed. We must keep in mind that the measurements are of the city only. There will be much more to Heaven.

The city of God will be pure gold (verse 18). In this world, people will kill and steal to obtain gold. In that city, God's people will walk on it!

There will be no temple in Heaven (verse 22). The earthly temples represented the place where God and man could meet. The Divine presence will be everywhere in that city. The entire city will feature the presence of God.

"The glory of God did lighten it, and the Lamb is the light thereof" (verse 23). This is why there will be no night there. Jesus is not only the light of the world (John 8:12), but He will be the light of Heaven as well. Jesus will outshine them all. *"The Lord shall be thine everlasting light"* (Isaiah 60:20).

National identity will apparently be maintained. *"And the nations of them which are saved shall walk in the light of it: and the kings of the earth do bring their glory and honour into it"* (verses 24,26). All honor and glory will go to King Jesus.

No sin will ever enter the eternal kingdom (verse 27). Sin is the thing that has spoiled this earth. If God let sin into Heaven, it would become like earth all over. Only those whose names are written in the Lamb's book of life will be permitted to enter. Once our name is inscribed there, it can never be removed (Revelation 3:5). The lost dead will not be found in the book of life (Revelation 20:12).

IV. Paradise Regained (Revelation 22:1-5)

The Word of God begins and ends with basically the same type of setting. The first two chapters of Genesis focus on creation and a paradise which was lost. These final two chapters of Revelation reveal the re-creation and paradise regained.

"And he shewed me a pure river of water of life...proceeding out of the throne of God and of the Lamb" (verse 1). Water has played a significant role in the history of man. Most major cities are located near large bodies of water.

The Garden of Eden had a river (Genesis 2:10). The crystal clear river that is in Heaven does not spring up from the ground, but flows from the throne of God and the Lamb. The source of refreshment is the throne of God. All our blessings come from Him.

This heavenly stream is the real Fountain of Youth. It is called "water of life". This means that it is "living" or "running" water. It reminds us of Jesus' statement to the woman at the well, *"Whosoever drinketh of the water that I shall give him shall never thirst"* (John 4:14).

This river will remind us of the Holy Spirit (John 7:37-39). It will be a "pure river", unlike the polluted streams of this world.

We learn there is water in Heaven, but will we be able to eat? *"On either side of the river...tree of life...twelve manner of fruits...leaves of the tree were for the healing of the nations"* (verse 2). Apparently, we will not have to eat, but food will be available for us.

The Tree of Life reminds us of the Garden of Eden. Adam was forbidden to eat of it or else he would have lived forever in an unredeemed body (Genesis 3:22-24). Overcomers had earlier been promised that they could eat of the tree of life (Revelation 2:7).

Please note that the tree of the knowledge of good and evil will not be found in Heaven. Man will never again be tempted to follow Satan. The devil is being tormented in the lake of fire. He will never be able to get out and deceive God's creatures again.

The leaves of the tree of life will be used for the "healing of the nations." The word for "healing" here means "health." It means that relationships between nations will be healed. There will be no more wars and fighting.

"And there shall be no more curse" (verse 3). The curse was because of Adam's sin (Genesis 3:17). This is why we have earthquakes, briars, thorns, etc. All of creation was affected by Adam's fall.

"His servants shall serve Him." There will be activity in Heaven. We won't strum on a harp or lay around and sleep. There will be things to do. Before the fall, Adam was the CEO of the Garden. He had responsibilities, but it wasn't work.

Heaven will be the most exciting place you have ever seen. The One who never makes an identical snowflake will provide plenty of variety for us.

"And they shall see His face" (verse 4). We can't look at Him directly now because we are sinners and He is holy. No person has yet seen God in His full glory ((I John 4:12). Being able to look at Him means we will have unbroken communion.

"His name shall be in their foreheads." We will be sealed for eternity. *"The foundation of God standeth sure, having this seal, the Lord knoweth them that are His"* (II Timothy 2:19). We are sealed now by the Holy Spirit (Ephesians 4:30).

The seal speaks of ownership and possession. The church is the bride of Christ and the bride will proudly take the name of her groom.

"And there shall be no night there" (verse 5). There will be no need for sleep because our bodies there will not be under the curse. Our spiritual bodies will never grow weary.

V. God's Final Words to Man (Revelation 22:6-21)

Final words are important to us. We have recorded here the closing invitation from God to mankind. We know His words are *"faithful and true"* (verse 6). Jesus had earlier identified Himself as *"the faithful and true witness"* (Revelation 3:14).

The word "quickly" is used three times in this section (verses 7, 12, 20). The word didn't mean that the Lord would return in a few years. It means suddenly. He will come in the twinkling of an eye (I Corinthians 15:52). Once the process of judgment begins, things will move rapidly to a conclusion.

John once again gets so excited that he fell down to worship the angel that had shown him these coming events (verse 8). The angel reminds the aged apostle that only God is to be worshiped (verse 9).

The gospel writers record several incidents in which individuals fell down to worship Jesus and none were ever rebuked. This is further proof that Jesus and God are One (John 10:30).

Have you ever wondered why Hell must be forever? Doesn't it seem that God could release the wicked at some point? The answer is given in verse 11. *"He that is unjust, let him be unjust still: and he which is filthy, let him be filthy still."* This verse is saying that character is permanently molded in this life and will never change in eternity.

Some have the idea if a drunk were to be let out of Hell that they would be in church Sunday morning. The truth is they would go right back to the liquor store. No one in Hell will ever repent. As death finds us, so shall we ever be.

Jesus described Hell as being a place where there would be *"gnashing of teeth"* (Matthew 8:12). The idea given here is one of rage against God. People in Hell will still hate God. Thus, they must remain there forever.

In contrast, those who love Jesus will love Him forever. *"He that is righteous, let him be righteous still: and he that is holy, let him be holy still."*

"Behold, I come quickly; and my reward is with me" (verse 12). The Lord will bring rewards when He comes. The Bible speaks of them as crowns. He will repay us for our service to Him after we were saved. How much will your check be?

"Blessed are they that do His commandments, that they may have right to the tree of life" (verse 14). The New Testament was translated out of Greek. The Greek here is better interpreted as "those who wash their robes." No one will be saved by keeping the commandments.

Verse 15 repeats a listing of those who will be shut out of the heavenly city. We saw Hell's neighborhood earlier (Revelation 21:8).

Jesus verifies the Book of Revelation (verse 16). He is telling us to teach this prophetic book in the church. One of the most beautiful titles for Him is given here as well. He is "the bright and morning star". The "morning star" appears just before dawn. This old world looks pretty dark right now, but the forecast is the Son will shine forever. The return of Christ is the only hope for this troubled world.

"Whosoever will, let him take the water of life freely" (verse 17). This entire Word of God could be summarized in the word "come." This has been God's call through the ages.

Strict warnings are given in verses eighteen and nineteen. We are commanded not to add to nor take away from the Holy Bible.

"If any man shall add unto these things, God shall add unto him the plagues that are written in this book." There is

a curse pronounced on those who would add to God's Word. There has not been a God-breathed book since Revelation.

"If any man shall take away...God shall take away his part out of the book of life" (verse 19). If we subtract from the Bible, we also will be under divine judgment. No true Child of God would do this anyway. These are warnings against the cults who claim their books to be equally inspired with the Bible.

"Surely I come quickly" (verse 20). This is the last promise in the Bible. John is also homesick for Heaven. "Even so, come, Lord Jesus".

"The grace of our Lord Jesus Christ be with you all" (verse 21). This is the last prayer in the holy scriptures.

Conclusion: The New Testament closes by talking about His return. We should also be homesick for Heaven. The Bible makes it clear that this world is not our home. Unless we are in the Rapture, we will soon go the way of all the earth. However, this will not be the end for us. *"Unto them that look for Him shall He appear the second time"* (Hebrews 9:28).

God's Blueprint for the future has been on the drawing board for many centuries. Soon the Divine Architect and Contractor will return and bring down the curtain on the stage of history.

Bibliography

Barnhouse, Donald Grey. *Revelation*. Grand Rapids, Mi.: Zondervan, 1971.

De Haan, M.R. *Revelation*. Grand Rapids, Mi.: Zondervan, 1946.

Gaebelein, Arno C. *The Revelation: An Exposition*. Neptune, N.J.: Loizeaux Bros., 1961.

Greene, Oliver B. *The Revelation: Verse by Verse Study*. Greenville, S.C.: Gospel Hour, 1963.

Hyles, Jack. *Let's Study the Revelation*. Murfreesboro, Tn.: Sword of the Lord, 1967.

Ironside, H.A. *Lectures on the Book of Revelation*. Neptune, N.J.: Loizeaux Bros., 1920.

LaHaye, Tim F. *Revelation Illustrated and Made Plain*. Grand Rapids, Mi.: Zondervan, 1973.

Lindsey, Hal. *There's A New World Coming*. Irvine, Ca.: Harvest House, 1973

Strauss, Lehman. *The Book of the Revelation*. Neptune, N.J.: Loizeaux Bros. 1964.